T0253177

WHY YOU SHOULD (OR SHOULDN'T) GO TO COLLEGE

No matter who you are or what your background might be, deciding whether or not to go to college, and which college to attend, is a complex and often stressful process. *Why You Should (or Shouldn't) Go to College* is written to help you become more informed and more comfortable in your decision-making so that perhaps some of the unavoidable anxiety is reduced, your questions are answered, and you can move forward confidently toward your goal … whatever it might be.

Full of easy-to-understand data and background on higher education and current economic workforce trends, this book provides an overview of the college process, including academic keywords and jargon, alternative routes, and "Student Silhouette" stories from others who have chosen a variety of paths post high school. This book will enhance your knowledge and choices when deciding what path is right for you.

Whether you are a stressed high school student trying to decide what's next, a parent deliberating your child's future, or a non-traditional student following your own path, this book has the knowledge and information needed to make deliberate and informed choices about your future education and career choices

Catherine G. Cordova has over a decade of experience leading and teaching within higher education at public university and community college settings. She has designed and overseen various innovative programs to assist students in their transition to college and is a certified career coach with a background in new student programming, orientation, first-generation research, and student engagement initiatives. She holds a Ph.D. in Curriculum and Instruction concentrated in Career and Workforce Education from the University of South Florida, USA.

WHY YOU SHOULD (OR SHOULDN'T) GO TO COLLEGE

A MODERN GUIDE FOR UNDERSTANDING YOUR COLLEGE AND CAREER CHOICES

Catherine Gorman Cordova, Ph.D.

NEW YORK AND LONDON

Designed cover image: © Getty Images

First published 2025
by Routledge
605 Third Avenue, New York, NY 10158

and by Routledge
4 Park Square, Milton Park, Abingdon, Oxon, OX14 4RN

Routledge is an imprint of the Taylor & Francis Group, an informa business

ISBN: 978-1-032-69222-7 (pbk)
ISBN: 978-1-032-69225-8 (ebk)

DOI: 10.4324/9781032692258

Typeset in Bembo
by Deanta Global Publishing Services, Chennai, India

TABLE OF CONTENTS

PREFACE

If you are holding this book, my guess is that you are a stressed high school student getting ready to attend college, but you are not sure what to study or where to go.

Should you even go?

Or, perhaps you are a stressed parent, afraid your child will never get a "good" job if they do not go to college.

It is possible that you are a returning student who took time off after high school, or who never finished college, but now want to learn more about the college environment and what to expect as you take the leap into higher education.

Maybe you are a "non-traditional student" whose pathway in education was not as well-defined as others, and now you are considering alternative education options while active in the workforce.

You could also be a parent wondering exactly what your tuition dollars are being used for, at alarmingly increasing rates.

No matter why you are holding this book, its purpose remains the same: to help you decipher your college and career selection process. No matter who you are or what your background might be, deciding whether or not to go to college, and which college to attend, is a complex and often stressful process. *Why You Should (or Shouldn't) Go to College* is written to help you become more informed and more comfortable in your decision-making so that perhaps some of the unavoidable anxiety is reduced, your questions are answered, and you can move forward confidently toward your goal … whatever it might be.

Having spent my current career in higher education, at a four-year public university and at a two-year community college, and being a certified career coach with a Ph.D. in Curriculum and Instruction concentrated in Career and Workforce Education, I continue to learn about higher education and the workforce daily. As a lifelong learner, I want to use my experiences as a student, faculty member, and administrator in higher education to help you decide whether or not college is right for you.

As a first-generation college student (the first in my immediate family to earn a four-year college degree), I feel as though too much of the college process is assumed intuitive, when none of it really is. I am blessed to have two hardworking parents who have always encouraged me to pursue my goals without pushing me into their contrived expectations. Still, when it came to college, their guidance was doing their best to lovingly support me and help in ways they knew while, learning alongside me about things we didn't know. Understanding the college process is tricky, and if you are fortunate enough to find a mentor to help offer guidance and decoding, the process can be far less intimidating and in many ways, rewarding.

Therefore, my goal with this text is to decode some of the mystique and misconceptions that surround the college process. I want to help you navigate the jargon that is rife in higher education, while giving you a realistic look at the workforce and whether or not college is a good choice for *your* goals. There are many pathways to a career, and at the end of the day, higher education is not for everyone – but it also was not designed to be. I want to pay forward all of the mentors who took the time to explain something about college to me, so that I could reach and achieve my goals. I wrote this book to share some of what I have learned in hopes of helping you, too.

This work is dedicated to my family, friends, mentors, teachers, and all those who took the time to guide me, support me, and help me succeed in college and throughout my career in higher education – especially Sean K. Kelly, Ph.D. To my first and always teachers, my parents, thank you. Special thanks also to Mitchell L. Cordova, Ph.D., for his love, support, and contributions to this work.

THE CURRENT COLLEGE AND CAREER CLIMATE

ABSTRACT

Chapter 1 presents a brief overview and data from what The Burning Glass Institute has termed "The Emerging Degree Reset" (2022). This chapter highlights some current workforce and economic trend data while discussing considerations surrounding higher education preparation for employment. Chapter 1 explains that while the labor market and education system are not mutually exclusive, there are opportunities in both. This chapter encourages students to consider all options when deciding whether or not to attend college and offers this text as a resource for informing their decision.

THE CURRENT FORECAST ... YOU MIGHT WANT YOUR UMBRELLA

The college and workplace environments are changing. Student enrollments are decreasing throughout higher education post-pandemic (Sedmak, 2020). What was once considered a necessary step for career preparation has begun to shift to a place of political infighting, high debt, and what some consider childlike coddling (Lukianoff & Haidt, 2018). With fewer students attending college and considering whether or not a degree is valuable (Jaschik, 2023), it is no surprise that colleges and universities spend so much time and energy on first-year programming to retain their current students. In fact, most universities have entire departments within

DOI: 10.4324/9781032692258-1

Student Affairs dedicated to the First Year Experience (FYE), specifically designed to help students transition and feel a sense of belonging in their new educational environments.

Although the college process can be challenging to navigate, higher education remains the expected and anticipated progression for most students following high graduation. Colleges and universities allow for augmented education, inspiration, resources, access, and future income. Data supports that college dropouts have a nearly 20% increased risk of unemployment and earn 32.6% less in average income in comparison to those who earn Bachelor's degrees (Hanson, 2022). Given this data, college is and should remain a goal for many students with specific career aspirations … but it may not be the right choice for *every* student.

Though it has deviated significantly from its foundation, higher education is rooted in the liberal arts education tenants of grammar, logic, and rhetoric, known as the Trivium (National Academy of Sciences, 2018). Early education is attributed to classical thinkers such as Socrates, Plato, Saint Augustine of Hippo, Jean-Jacques Rousseau, Matthew Arnold, Thomas Huxley, and Saint Thomas Aquinas (Glaude, 2017; Kimball, 1986; Rose, 2015). And though once aimed at teaching general and holistic transferrable skills, American higher education is now deemed responsible for helping tens of thousands of students each year graduate and find a job. In fact, 88% of college freshman cited getting a good job as their main motivation for attending college (The Chronicle of Higher Education, 2022).

BUT DO YOU REALLY NEED A COLLEGE EDUCATION IN ORDER TO BE EMPLOYED?

The answer is undoubtedly, no. In fact, although more than half of adults believe college education is important, the percentage has declined markedly from 70% to 51% in the last decade (Marken, 2019). Those who do still feel college is necessary see it as a means to an end, where better job prospects is the gain (The Burning Glass Institute, 2022). However, many adults are very successful without a college degree; and just because someone holds a college degree does not mean that they will automatically land their dream job and it certainly does not guarantee success. According to Gallup poll data, fewer than half of all college graduates feel as though they are employed in purposeful work (Marken, 2019).

To add to the dilemma, in what The Burning Glass Institute has termed "The Emerging Degree Reset" (2022), it has been estimated that over the next 5 years, 1.4 million jobs will be opening without requiring a college degree from applicants. This is especially good news for the 64% of working-age adults who do not hold four-year college degrees (The Burning Glass Institute, 2022). The changing perception of the value of degrees coupled with the dynamic workforce prediction that 85% of jobs that will be in demand in 2030 do not even exist yet, makes one question the value of a current degree (Dell Technologies & IFTF, 2023).

For those who do pursue college, more than 25% do not return for their second year (NSCRC, 2022). In the community college environment, this retention rate is even worse, with 41% of students not returning to complete their degree (NSCRC, 2022). Likewise, according to the National Student Clearing House, over 39 million American adults have completed some college with no credentials, and the number continues to increase. Perhaps what is more striking is that only a little more than 62% complete college within 6 years (NSCRC, 2022). This means that fewer adults than in the past believe college is necessary, and many of those who go to college do not feel as though their achieved careers are purposeful.

SO WHAT GIVES?

Within my time in higher education, it has become clear that there is a growing trend and an evident gap in what students expect colleges and universities to provide and what they actually experience in outcome. Many students come to college expecting to be taught how to build a career within a certain field and anticipate a degree in the field to serve as a qualifying entry point. For example, business majors often think that if they get a degree in business they will learn everything there is to know about owning and running a successful business … though any business owner would likely balk at this notion, claiming that they learned by on-the-job training. Still, business degrees are some of the most popularly sought in higher education, so it is not so far-fetched to assume that the business owner who balks at the business major likely holds a four-year degree themselves, without valuing it from their employees. This cycle is contributing to the declining value perception of college degrees. During the COVID-19 pandemic, this was especially true. With the shift to online instruction, college enrollment, and completion rates fell (NSCRC, 2023), and over half of college students reported feeling as though they learned less than in prior years, with 47% going so far as to rate their educational experience as fair or poor (Ezarik, 2021). It is no secret that across the U.S., the cost of college tuition inflation has increased over 12% annually in the past 10 years and a whopping 747.8% since 1963 (Hanson, 2023), with college debt rates soaring at even greater extents. Why would you pay all that money for a degree when you may not be happy in your classes and may not feel fulfilled in your future career?

THE ANSWER IS SIMPLE …

Just like all decisions in life, college comes with opportunity, cost, and risk. Within American society, we love to champion those who became billionaires without college degrees – individuals like Mark Zuckerberg, Michael Dell, and Steve Jobs who founded high-tech conglomerates. Nevertheless, census data supports that the majority of business owners hold a Baccalaureate degree, and key findings from Georgetown University's Center on Education and the Workforce report that full-time, full-year employees with a four-year degree can expect to earn 84% more over the course of their lifetime than an individual with a high school diploma (Carnevale et al., 2011). Yet, the higher earnings should be balanced against the fact that many jobs that once required only a two-year degree or high school diploma are now being inflated to a four-year degree or more (Fain, 2017); and it can be assumed that those who paid for their four-year degrees incurred more debt than those who only spent two years in college. In other words, a two-year degree may no longer qualify you for the same job it did before; so if you choose to attend college, you may need to anticipate paying for four years of schooling. Unfortunately, more recent trends show that various areas of study in higher education have shown salary decreases (NACE, 2022). So, although you may be spending more time and money in college, and gaining debt, you may graduate making less than others with the same degree or with no degree.

LEARNING AND GROWTH

Just as your decision to go to college or not has multiple influences, your outcome has lots of possibilities for learning and growth. The current trends and anticipated changes in the economic environment make the already stressful decision of deciding on college an even more daunting task. The labor force and education system are not mutually exclusive, so your decision is one that is inspired by a variety of factors. "College" is an overarching term that encompasses various opportunities and parts of higher education, so choosing a college means broadening your options and choices.

This book is meant to help you determine whether or not college is the right choice for *you*. It offers some realistic data and research related to the current state of higher education, particularly given the influence of the COVID-19 pandemic and changes in the economy and inflationary economic trends. Although it is written by "an academic," this text is not meant to sway your decision toward any particular path; rather, it is intended to educate you so that your final decision is an informed one. As Sir Francis Bacon famously quoted, "Knowledge is power" (1597). Use this book to gain knowledge and empower one of the most important decisions of your life. Good luck!

REFERENCES

Bacon, F. (1597). *Meditationes sacrae.* Excusum impensis Humfredi Hooper.

Carnevale, A. P., Strohl, J., & Melton, M. (2011). What's it worth? The economic value of college majors. Georgetown University Center on Education and the Workforce. https://cew.georgetown.edu/wp-content/uploads/2014/11/ whatsitworth-complete.pdf

Dell Technologies & Institute for the Future (IFTF). (2023). Realizing 2030: A divided vision of the future. Dell Technologies. https://www.delltechnologies.com/content/dam/delltechnologies/assets/perspectives/2030/pdf/Realizing-2030-A-Divided-Vision-of-the-Future-Summary.pdf

Ezarik, M. (2021). How COVID-19 damaged student success. *Inside Higher Ed.* https://www.insidehighered.com/news/2021/06/21/what-worked-and-what-didn%E2%80%99t-college-students-learning-through-covid-19#:~:text=More%20than%20half%20(52%20percent,somewhat%20common%20in%20online%20courses

Fain, P. (2017). College degrees lead to "Good Jobs." *Inside Higher Ed.* https://www.insidehighered.com/news/2017/07/26/increasing-share-good-paying-jobs-go-college-graduates

Glaude, Jr. E. S. (2017). AAR Presidential address: A liberal arts education in the age of Trump. *Journal of the American Academy of Religion, 86*(2), 297–396. https://doi:10.1093/jaarel/lfy()03

Hanson, M. (2022). College dropout rates. Education Data Initiative. https://educationdata.org/college-dropout-rates/

Hanson, M. (2023). College tuition inflation. Education Data Initiative. https://educationdata.org/college-tuition-inflation-rate

Jaschik, S. (2023). Why students opt not to enroll. *Inside Higher Ed.* https://www.insidehighered.com/news/admissions/2023/06/12/why-students-opt-out-college?utm_source=Inside+Higher+Ed&utm_campaign=8f4624a2fb-DNU_2021_COPY_02&utm_medium=email&utm_term=0_1fcbc04421-8f4624a2fb-237827861&mc_cid=8f4624a2fb&mc_eid=5176a715a3

Kimball, B. A. (1986). *Orators & philosophers: A history of liberal arts education.* Teachers College Press.

Lukianoff, G., & Haidt, J. (2018). *The Coddling of the American mind: How good intentions and bad ideas are setting up a generation for failure.* Penguin Press.

Marken, S. (2019). Half in U.S. now consider college education very important. Gallup, Inc. https://www.gallup.com/education/272228/half-consider-college-education-important.aspx

National Association of Colleges & Employers (NACE). (2022). First destinations for the college class of 2021. Findings and analysis. NACE.

National Student Clearinghouse Research Center (NSCRC). (2022). More than 39 million Americans have some college, no credential, according to new research. National Student Clearinghouse. https://www.studentclearinghouse.org/more-than-39-million-americans-have-some-college-no-credential-according-to-new-research/

National Student Clearinghouse Research Center (NSCRC). (2023). Undergraduate degree earners. Academic year 2021–2022. National Student Clearinghouse. https://nscresearchcenter.org/undergraduate-degree-earners/

Rose, M. (2015). The liberal arts and the virtues. A Thomistic history. *Logos, 34–65.* https://doiorg.ezproxy.lib.usf.edu/10.1353/log.2015.0017

Sedmak, T. (2020). Fall 2020 undergraduate enrollment down 4% compared to same time last year. National Student Clearinghouse. https://www.stu dentclearing house.org/blog/fall-2020-undergraduate-enrollment-down-4-compared-to-same-time-last-year/

The Burning Glass Institute. (2022). The Emerging degree reset. How the shift to skills-based hiring holds the keys to growing the U.S. workforce at a time of talent shortage. The Burning Glass Institute.

The Chronicle of Higher Education. (2022). *Building tomorrow's work force. What employers want you to know.* The Chronicle of Higher Education, Inc.

The National Academy of Sciences. (2018). *The integration of the humanities and arts with sciences, engineering, and medicine in higher education: Branches from the same tree.* The National Academies Press. https://doi.org/10.17226/24988

COLLEGE AND CAREER SUCCESS SKILLS

ABSTRACT

Chapter 2 outlines the NACE career-readiness competencies while providing data related to employment skills. The chapter provides guidance for all students (those who choose college and those who do not) on writing a cover letter and résumé/CV. It highlights some of the gaps in workplace expectations and encourages students to research their future jobs and begin taking steps toward their careers. Chapter 2's Student Silhouette is an example of a student who used their personal skills to help define their future career goals.

THE HARD (SKILLS) TRUTH

Whether you choose to go directly into the workforce, or to go to college, it is important that you are prepared for the career you are seeking. Your future goals should include not just a job provided by a college degree or otherwise, but a career with advancement opportunities and salary pay so that you can make long-term, livable wages. These types of careers require industry knowledge and what might be considered "hard" skills, or skills directly applicable to the industry. Although 66% of higher education students believed that they had the necessary critical analytical employment skills, only 26% of employers agreed (Long, 2018). Career skill development is critical to your future success. Perhaps this is why many employers are now offering what is known as **upskilling**, **cross-skilling**, and **reskilling**. In an effort to invest in the career development of their employees, employers may provide training to upskill – or teach necessary industry skills – to their current employees rather than hire new ones. Rather than bear the cost of replacing an employee – which can range from one-half to two-times an annual salary, organizations are using upskilling as a means of reducing turnover (McFeely & Wigert, 2019). Cross-skilling is another employee retainment strategy that occurs through employer-motivated colleague collaboration meant to help an employee in one area of the industry learn the skills necessary for another area. Similarly, reskilling moves an employee from one role within an organization to a new role with skill development support so that they can learn that area (ITA Group, 2023). Employers are increasing their focus on employee skill development, especially within skilled labor jobs, to help recruit, retain, and invest more in the careers of their employees. Although you can benefit from these career skill strategies while employed, you can increase your employability overall and equip yourself with the necessary skills long before you apply for a job.

BE CAREER READY

The National Association of Colleges and Employers (NACE) defines career readiness using eight key competencies: Critical Thinking/Problem Solving, Oral/Written Communications, Teamwork/Collaboration, Digital Technology, Leadership, Professionalism/Work Ethic, Career Management, and Global/ Intercultural Fluency (NACE, 2021). Whether you graduate from high school or college, you should make sure you are aware of these skills before entering the workplace. This will make you more employable. As a student in high school, technical school, or college, you have had opportunities to work in teams, demonstrate leadership, communicate orally and by written means, problem solve, and critically think. You have also been exposed to diversity to increase your global/intercultural fluency. *All* of these skills should therefore be on your résumé to show future employers all you have to offer. One career skill that is especially important to your employment success is the NACE competency, Professionalism/ Work Ethic: 97.5% of surveyed employers cited Professionalism/ Work Ethic as "Essential" or "Absolutely Essential" for student career readiness (NACE, 2021). Students who exhibit this skill are present, prepared, meet goals, pay attention to details, are dedicated to a job, and have integrity and accountability to self, others, and their organization (NACE, 2021).

You may think that college students have an advantage in Professionalism/Work Ethic skills (or any of the other competencies); however, this is not the case. You can be very successful in your chosen career if you skip college but still possess these qualities. Also, do not assume colleges are teaching them. Many university degrees require capstone courses or projects that are aimed at producing a final piece of student-created material to support learned career competencies and skills. Unfortunately, these courses are often left until students' final year in college, taking for granted the fact that many students have not been taught how to write a cover letter or format a résumé. Thus, whether you attend college or go directly into the workforce, you can make yourself more marketable by demonstrating career-readiness skills.

LET'S BE CLEAR …

When applying for a job, someone who is without a college degree but who has professional skills and a desire to learn is often far more marketable than someone with a college degree but no demonstrable skills and the need for professional training. Skills and experiences are recorded on a résumé or a **curriculum vitae (CV)**. A CV is very similar to a résumé, but it is much longer and includes a comprehensive list of work and credentials. This is more commonly used in academia than in businesses, so be sure to provide whichever is required.

Since résumés are most commonly needed when applying for a job, here are some simple tips for you:

1.) A résumé should generally only be two pages long and should include jobs *and* skills/responsibilities/certifications. Be sure to include any volunteer work as well.
2.) Résumés should be chronological so that your current or most recent job and work is at the top and your most outdated work is at the bottom.
3.) If you do not have on-the-job experience in the field for which you are applying, you should volunteer to gain related skills. If

you are unable to volunteer, you can list job shadowing or even related coursework that you have taken.

4.) Be sure to include all credentials and education at the top of your résumé so that the employer knows right away that you meet the standard qualifications.

5.) Use active and professional words when describing your work. These should be things such as "Managed cleanliness of produce section of a grocery store" not "Swept and mopped the produce section of a store." Both are good tasks and skills to have, but "managing cleanliness" is a better way of stating it on a résumé.

6.) As you continue gaining experience and building your résumé, you can remove irrelevant information or outdated jobs to allow for new career-related skills and experiences.

Along with submitting a résumé for a job, you should include a cover letter – even if it is not required. Why? For one thing, it instantly demonstrates your writing abilities. Second, it shows that you took the time to research a bit about the job for which you are applying.

Here are some simple cover letter tips for you:

1. Research a job at an employer for which you would like to work in the future and make note of the listed qualifications and responsibilities.

2. Research the organization, its mission, and its vision. Be sure they align with your future goals.

3. Begin writing your cover letter.

4. Remember that a cover letter should generally not be more than two pages long and should include the following in order:
   a. State the exact job for which you are applying (i.e., "I am applying for the Manager of Sales position at …").
   b. Specifically, state why you believe you are a good fit for the company (i.e., "I believe my previous experience matches the qualifications you are seeking and believe in your organization's mission of …").
   c. State any current qualifications you hold for the position.
   d. State any future qualifications you will have or believe would contribute to your success (i.e., "I will be completing

a certificate in software engineering in March and believe this will help contribute to my success with your organization as I continue learning from your team.").

e. Subtly praise the company and be humble (i.e., "I would love to work for an organization that has it in its mission to respect the environment and would like to learn and contribute to this cause.").

f. End with "I look forward to hearing back from you" with your contact information.

Remember that cover letters are your *first* opportunity to impress your future employer, so be sure to check for grammar, spelling, and professionalism. If you do not feel these are strengths you possess, ask a mentor or counselor to review your résumé and cover letter before submitting. You can also utilize career services on your college campus or public career service centers in your community. Also, do not be afraid to drop off your résumé and cover letter at the business of your dreams even if they aren't hiring. You can ask the company to keep it on file should they begin hiring in the near future. This shows incredible initiative and is one more way in which you can stand out as a candidate for their company.

BE CAREER PREPARED

Notice that one of the main tasks in applying for a job is preparing by researching the company to which you are applying. Begin by researching individuals and credentials of those in the field in which you are interested in order to find out the necessary requirements. Searching LinkedIn profiles of those within a desired organization and doing an online search of career platforms that offer salary and qualification information are all good ways you can explore career requirements. If you want to pursue an **internship** with a specific organization, you can reach out through a professional introductory email by stating why you are interested in the field and inquiring whether or not they offer internships. Of course, be sure to include your résumé. This is a good way to begin networking and gain early access to a field. If a paid internship is not possible, you can ask to shadow a job or interview an executive to learn more about the workplace environment. Once again, this offers a low-risk opportunity for learning and experience with quality networking; it can also provide information about specific job qualifications. Additionally, online resources such as Career Coach, hosted by Emsi, provide job overviews, wages, necessary qualifications, similar careers, and live job postings. You can also complete a career assessment designed to help narrow down skills and interests. Although the results may be broad, they can still provide some researchable ideas.

Perhaps what is most useful in researching future jobs with online tools is the opportunity to see what percentage of practitioners hold certain degrees. For example, fast research through Career Coach displays a median salary for veterinarians of $103,358 annually; but, 91% of those in the field have a Doctoral degree or more, with 9% holding a Master or professional degree (Career Coach, 2023). Conversely, researching the audio and video technicians field reveals a median salary of $38,650 annually, with 43% of practitioners holding a Bachelor degree, 25% holding a high school diploma or less, and 20% practicing with a certificate (Career Coach, 2023).

Gasp! There is a big difference between a $103,358 salary and a $38,650 salary. However, you are smart enough to now consider the cost of tuition. College is expensive and veterinarians have approximately ten years' worth of tuition to pay for their degree and qualifications. Audio visual technicians, however, have far less required schooling and much less educational qualification debt. Research suggests that 64% of Americans believe that pursuing a college degree is worth doing … so long as it does not produce large amounts of debt (Moran, 2019). This could be because 43.6 million individuals are currently facing US federal student loan debt, with an average balance of almost $40,000 (Hanson, 2023). Suddenly the impressive salary feels daunting with ten years of tuition bills.

It would be unwise to suggest a veterinarian give up their lifelong dream simply because they will incur debt and endure a decade of higher education. However, the comparison is effective in demonstrating that certain careers may not require the same educational commitment as others; and if you are not interested in participating in any schooling, there are many occupations that remain good options. Take welding, for example: welding positions require a high school diploma or less as education requirements, but offer an in-demand, sustainable, livable career (BLS, 2022). Likewise, working as a machinist, a carpenter, a marine mechanic, or a technician can offer a comfortable quality of life and a consistent career. Similarly, working as an emergency medical technician (EMT), a firefighter, or a police officer can be obtained with a certificate and provide a stable career with promotion opportunities, benefits, and a good salary. Furthermore, fields in technology are some of the highest paying jobs with diverse qualifications ranging from a high school diploma to graduate degrees; yet they allow for strong advancement and remain high on the US Bureau Labor Statistics growth employment projections (BLS, 2022). Depending on your interests, your job may or may not require a degree.

KNOW WHAT YOU'RE GETTING INTO

Within the post global pandemic context, the need for secure employment has perhaps not seemed as necessary since the U.S. Great Depression. The current health environment has brought about necessary changes in distancing, awareness, and sanitation in both personal and professional practices. Likewise, the daily workplace is adapting to virtual transactions dependent upon the technology STEM fields boast about providing. Over 50% of employees found their work disrupted and changed due to the pandemic (DeLollis, 2021). Employers, too, had to adapt. Job postings that once required Bachelor's degrees declined from 35% to 23%, including education qualifications for nurses (Fuller et al., 2022). Within this new environment, students have begun exploring and pursuing less time-intensive, non-traditional education options such as stackable credits, skill development boot camps, and hybrid education programs (DeLollis, 2021). Be sure to explore all of the necessary training and credentialing options you need to be as highly skilled, knowledgeable, and marketable as possible in your future career choice.

What is perhaps most pivotal in your workplace decision is your future job satisfaction. Being satisfied in a career has been well-researched and supports that it is positively linked to employee loyalty, productivity, and overall improvements (Aziri, 2011). This reinforces the idea that if you enjoy your work you will be far happier and more productive. I would posit the same applies to life! If you enjoy the environment, you are far more likely to be successful in the setting. Ultimately, choosing to forego college in pursuit of a career is a personal decision. Parents may expect it, enforce it, and finance it – but research does not support that college education equals job correlation 100% of the time. In fact, current college dropout rates demonstrate that only about 67% of undergraduate students complete their degrees, with about 33% dropping out before their fourth year (Hanson, 2022). Think of all of the tuition fees that could have been saved!

So if you are eager to sit in a classroom, read, research, and build college academic skills, then college is a good option. However, if you want to get on a job site or climb into an attic exploring HVAC, the college or university is not the right environment or does not promote learning and growth for you, personally. The costs outweigh the benefits in a very tangible and fiscal way. Take the time to decide whether or not pursuing a four-year university degree really is the best choice for you after high school and be confident knowing that education is an ongoing process. Even if you don't go to college, you still have learning to do and a market-able skillset that can afford you a happy and fulfilling career.

STUDENT SILHOUETTE: KEVIN

I always wanted to be a doctor and thought that medical school was my goal. After my first two years in college, I realized that I had no interest in my biology classes, or even really college. I stuck it out for two more years and finished my degree but changed to business (much to the disappointment of my mother). I thought if I completed a business degree I would have an idea about what I wanted to do and could work pretty much anywhere since all jobs were "businesses." Unfortunately, I was wrong.

My Bachelor's in business did not prove as valuable as I had hoped, because after graduation I had no job and no idea of what I wanted to do. I started working a part-time job at our local grocery and researched different careers. Even though I decided not to become a doctor, I was still interested in the medical field. I did some research related to other jobs in the hospital industry and found out that I could be a hospital administrator. I researched the necessary requirements and left my job at the grocery store for a part-time job as an office clerk at a hospital, which turned into a full-time job as an office manager. The hospital paid for me to complete two hospital certifications and I now have experience overseeing other employees and managing a budget. I volunteer for hospital functions every chance I get because it gives me the opportunity to network with administrators. I plan to ask to shadow one of them on my day off so that I see what "a day in the life" is really like. Hospital administrators can make a lot of money and I am hoping that beginning my career in an entry-level job at a respectable hospital will help me grow with them and continue finding opportunities.

The real-life experience in managing the office and networking at the hospital has provided me with more experience and learning than my degree ever did. I wish I had saved my money and figured out what I wanted to do sooner; but the truth is, I am not sure I would have known when I graduated high school. Working in the grocery store gave me skills that I use in my current job. It also gave me the motivation to research other jobs, which is how I found out about hospital administration.

I plan to keep learning the industry as an office manager and working toward more hospital administrator certifications. Even though I ended up in a career completely different than I thought, I am happy that I'm not a doctor and believe I will be a great hospital administrator someday.

REFERENCES

Aziri, B. (2011). Job satisfaction: A literature review. *Management Research & Practice*, *3*(4). https://journals.sagepub.com/doi/abs/10.1177/0734016808324230

Career Coach. (2023). Career coach. Emsi. www.fsw.emsicc.com

DeLollis, B. (2021). Preventing a "Lost Generation": Understanding education and work in a time of crisis. Strada. https://access.ihenow.com/preventing-a-lostgeneration-understanding-education-and-work-in-a-time-of crisis

Fuller, J., Langer, C., & Sigelman, M. (2022). Skills-based hiring is on the rise. Harvard Business Review. https://hbr.org/2022/02/skills-based-hiring-is-on-the-rise

Hanson, M. (2022). College dropout rates. Education Data Initiative. https://educationdata.org/college-dropout-rates/

Hanson, M. (2023). Student loan debt statistics. Education Data Initiative. https://educationdata.org/student-loan-debt-statistics

ITA Group. (2023). How upskilling your workforce benefits your organization. ITA Group. https://www.itagroup.com/insights/employee-experience/how-upskilling-your-workforce-benefits-your-organization

Long, J. R. (2018). *Critical thinking in context: An examination of how humanities faculty and prospective employers define and assess a broad career-readiness competency* (Doctoral dissertation). ProQuest Dissertations and Theses.

McFeely, S., & Wigert, B. (2019). This fixable problem costs U.S. businesses $1trillion. Gallup, Inc. https://www.gallup.com/workplace/247391/fixable-problem-costs-businesses-trillion.aspx

Moran, G. (2019). No, humanities degrees don't mean low salaries. *Forbes*. https://fortune.com/2019/12/10/humanities-degree-jobs-salaries/

National Association of Colleges & Employers (NACE). (2021). Career readiness defined. NACE. http://www.naceweb.org/careerreadiness/competencies/careerreadiness-defined/

The United States Census Bureau. (2022). A higher degree. U.S. Census Bureau, U.S. Department of Commerce. https://www.census.gov/library/visualizations/2022/comm/a-higher-degree.html

TRADITIONAL COLLEGE ALTERNATIVES AND CAREER OPTIONS

Vocational Degrees, Internships, Apprenticeships, Trade Schools, Skilled Jobs, and the Military

ABSTRACT

Chapter 3 discusses various options and opportunities related to the traditional college environment by sharing information, data, and resources related to vocational degrees, internships, apprenticeships, trade schools, skilled jobs, and the military. It also includes two "Student Silhouettes" featuring students who chose the military and a trade occupation over the traditional college experience.

IF YOU GO, WILL YOU STAY?

Consider this: you spent most of your high school career being told that in order to get into the college of your choice, you had to have a grade point average (**GPA**) of 3.0 or higher. Yet, almost half of high school graduates who accomplish this and then go to college never finish. Should they have ever gone in the first place? According to data, almost half (40%) of students who drop out of college have a 3.0 GPA or higher (Hanson, 2022). Additionally, 39% of students who dropped out of college cited feeling as though they weren't getting their money's worth as motivation for leaving (Hanson, 2022). This could all be due to the fact that almost a

DOI: 10.4324/9781032692258-3

quarter of all college freshmen report feeling as though they were underprepared for college (Ezarik, 2021) and a contributing factor as to why since 2019, there has been an 8% increase in high school students reporting not going to college simply because they do not find the degree valuable (Jaschik, 2023).

As evinced by the data, there remains a sharp contrast between what students expect higher education to provide and what they feel they receive. College has historically been viewed as the necessary passage to accessing "good" jobs with higher wages. Although this may be true in some cases, in what's been termed "The Emerging Degree Reset" (The Burning Glass Institute, 2022), fewer organizations are requiring degrees for employment and instead are seeking skills. This means that jobs that may have previously required degree qualifications are now seeking skills instead. The current economic and employment shift from degree-based hiring to skill-based hiring is not a new concept. Although it may seem like a symptom of the pandemic, the trend against "degree inflation" toward skills-based hiring began in the early 2000s (Fuller et al., 2022). Accordingly, from 2017 to 2019, 46% of middle-skill positions lessened their degree requirements – this was especially true within IT positions (Fuller et al., 2022). This is why you must research the necessary skills and qualifications related to those active in the career field of your choice – and if skills are more prominent than degrees, higher education may not be the right choice for you.

THE CTE OPTION

Thus, while considering your future education options, it may be in your best interest to pursue **career and technical education (CTE)**, also known as **vocational education**. Many high school curricula include optional academies and opportunities for you to begin earning industry credentials while earning your high school diploma. Likewise, career and technical schools/colleges provide a more realistic experience in preparing students for the work-force. Certain CTE programs offer **Associate of Occupational Studies (A.O.S.)** and **Associate of Applied Science (A.A.S.)** degrees that are unique and provide certifications within specific fields. Thus, when pursuing higher education at a vocational school or technical college, you can be sure that what you are learning in the classroom will be applied to your future job.

Rather than requiring general education classes with liberal arts backgrounds, vocational education schools teach students skills that can be directly applied to the workplace. CTE colleges and schools are wonderful options for students who prefer kinesthetic learning (physical learning) and hands-on training. What's more is that vocational schools often have partnerships with local businesses, thus allowing you to receive credentials while getting on-site experience. CTE classes are often offered outside of normal working hours to allow students to pursue their education alongside their careers. Different from traditional colleges and universities, though equally diverse, CTE colleges often include non-traditional learners and students who are dedicated to learning a trade. These learning environments may be trade schools, vocational/technical schools (vo-tech), or learning academies. They may be less interested in the socialization aspect of college and more interested in personal skill education and careers. Additionally, vocational schools offer courses and training for in-demand jobs, including **skilled** or **trade jobs**. CTE often costs less than a university, has a more flexible schedule, and teaches students about jobs with above-average pay given their need for aptitude and skills within the industry. Thus, when deciding on whether or not to attend a career college or a vocational school, it is important to consider *why* the pursuit is important to you and *how* this pursuit helps in achieving your personal and professional goals. What is your motivation?

Without question, certain careers require higher education degrees as minimal application requirements. Still, other careers can be obtained without college credits. Research indicates that you can apply your skills to make good wages without a degree as a legal assistant, bus or truck driver, brick mason, construction equipment operator, crane operator, wind turbine technician, diesel technician, plumber, home inspector, auto/transportation technician, landscape designer, pilot, and electrician (Indeed, 2023). What's more is that many of these jobs afford you promotional opportunities, on-site training, *high national average salaries,* and a consistent, stable, in-demand career.

THE APPRENTICESHIP OPTION

If you choose not to go to college preferring to begin your career, you will need to ensure that you begin building skills to make you marketable in the field. This can be done by job shadowing, consistent and meaningful volunteer work, and entry-level positions in the career or a related field. You can also complete an **apprenticeship**. Apprenticeships are on-the-job training (OJT) that provides mentorship, pay, credentials, and a structured plan for skill-building within the industry (ApprenticeshipUSA, 2023). Some of the main differences between internships/externships and apprenticeships are the amount of time and the structure of training. Internships and externships are generally a semester long since they are often connected to college credit. Similarly, internships and externships are opportunities to learn about an industry by being exposed to various skills and even multiple industries. Apprenticeships, on the other hand, are structured skill-building employment. They provide students with the opportunity to learn an industry and be paid to fill a specific need within the workforce, in what has become known as an "earn and learn" model (WINTAC, 2023). Sometimes apprenticeships may even begin in high school and include credentials and college credit as well. Certain apprenticeships may offer classroom training or reimbursement for certifications. According to the U.S. Department of Labor, there has been a 106% growth in apprenticeships offered in the U.S. over the last decade (ApprenticeshipUSA). This coincides with employers seeking more skilled labor; they can register hiring opportunities within their state and work with the Department of Education to find employees. With well over a half-million active apprenticeship opportunities in America, employers are actively seeking students to fill employment needs and positions for skilled jobs (ApprenticeshipUSA).

THE MILITARY OPTION

In addition to exploring vocational degrees, trade schools, and apprenticeships, you may also consider one of the most honorable ways of gaining both an education and career skills: *through the military.* Joining the military is perhaps one of the best ways to expose yourself to diverse learning environments, unique opportunities, and a guaranteed well-paying job. No matter the economic fluctuations, those in the military earn a consistent and well-earned wage for their work. You can enlist in the military during or after high school through the Reserve Officer's Training Corps (ROTC) or a local recruiter office. Those who join the military after high school set themselves apart: only 1% of Americans join the military after high school (USAA, 2022). If you enlist and choose to attend college following your military career, your G.I. Bill and military assistance program will cover the costs of your degree, books, healthcare, and possibly housing! You can also choose to join the military during or after college as an Officer rather than an enlisted member. Taking part in ROTC in college allows you to earn your degree while the military pays for it. Upon graduation, you will begin your career by learning skills alongside those protecting the freedoms we enjoy here in the U.S.

Deciding to pursue a military career instantly provides you with in-demand employment skills. Those in the military gain physical and emotional intelligence that is universally recognized by employers. These skills include: leadership, enhanced maturity, technical and tactical proficiency, decision-making, teamwork, occupational skills, problem-solving, responsibility, global awareness, and many more (VA, 2023). Rather than join your peers accruing college debt after high school, you might consider joining the military as a means of expanding your opportunities and guaranteeing your future employment skill development. A career in the military may also be appealing to you depending on your branch and passions. For example, if you enjoy aviation, the Air Force or Navy may be good choices. Likewise, if you want to travel on the sea, or enjoy working on planes, ships, or aircraft, the Navy or Merchant Marines have many opportunities. If you want to travel on land and fly drones or helicopters, the Marines or Army may be enjoyable for you. If you want to ride in or work on a tank, the Army can offer you experience. If you want to be on the water performing search and rescue or piloting ships, the Coast Guard or Merchant Marines should be a consideration. Each of these military options exposes you to diverse opportunities and in-demand skills that can be applied to a variety of fields and industries as a civilian.

Also, know that veterans qualify for GI Bill educational benefits and can even transfer their educational benefits to their spouse or dependents (VA, 2023). For this reason, it is important to note that a military occupation can directly transfer to college and university credits. In fact, the University of North Carolina has recently created a new roadmap tool called the Military Equivalency System to help update the American Council on Education (ACE) guide (Blake, 2024). This system provides almost 7,000 (with a projection of 10,000) college course equivalency credits for work and occupations done in the military (Blake, 2024). So, in addition to gaining employment skills, a military career can also offer college and university credits if those align with your future goals. Just like any career decision, take the time to research possibilities and determine options that fit your strengths, skills, and future employment interests.

Whether military or otherwise, choosing an alternative to the traditional college degree *can* certainly lead to success. Within the current labor market, 27% of occupations have actually reduced degree requirements, with fewer requiring four-year degrees (The Burning Glass Institute, 2022). Yes – 27%! Between 2017 and 2020, healthcare, finance, sales, information technology (IT), human resource management (HR), and construction were some of the most impacted fields reducing degree qualifications (The Burning Glass Institute, 2022).

FOLLOW YOUR HEART

It is true that certain areas of study and expertise are always going to be in demand given the changing economic landscape and workforce needs. However, what is perhaps more consistent are the in-demand skills across various jobs. Courses (whether college or otherwise) that teach students a broad range of skills directly correlate with employer needs. Therefore, it is important that you remain aware of the "soft," "core," "people," or "success" skills you can develop and list on your résumé. These include: problem-solving, critical thinking, leadership and communication (Angeles & Roberts, 2017; Cuseo et al., 2020; Dey & Cruzvergara, 2019). These crucial skills can be found in the "Employability Skills

Framework" provided by the U.S. Department of Education Office of Career and Technical Education, and in the NACE Career Competencies (2021). They are essential for your successful career employment (US DOE, 2020). Don't believe me? "More than 90% of employers rate written communication, critical thinking, and problem-solving as 'very important' for the job success of new labor market entrants" (Arum & Roska, 2011, p. 143). Likewise, "detail-oriented" skill requirements rose 10% between 2017 and 2019 (The Burning Glass Institute, 2022).

Over the past 30 years, the fastest-growing jobs in the United States have all had social/soft skill requirements (Ruggeri, 2019); and even amidst the COVID-19 global pandemic, communications, problem-solving, teamwork, and critical thinking have all remained in the top six most commonly requested job skills in employment postings (Fain, 2020). Some companies even go so far as to directly and intentionally recruit students from majors outside corresponding job titles, effectively making a college major irrelevant. Large, well-known organizations such as Fidelity, Vanguard, Morningstar, Dodge and Cox, Deloitte, and McKinsey, all seek out and employ graduates with diverse degrees, noting their skill transferability (Anders, 2017). This is why listing skills and experience alongside qualifications on your résumé is so important.

Even with so many employers seeking these core skills, there remains debate about whether or not colleges and universities provide the necessary education. As authors Seemiller and Grace explain:

> The desire for real-world preparation is echoed by more than one-third of business leaders who believe that higher education does not adequately help students develop critical skills necessary for the workplace.
> (2016, p. 219)

By choosing to forego or delay traditional college choices for a career, you are joining millions of others in the workforce. In doing so, you are expanding your options and opportunities. Remember that changing jobs, gaining education, building skills, learning training, and pursuing a different career are all options available to you. Take the time to assess your choice and determine what is next: Promotion? Entrepreneurship? College? Choosing not to attend a university may seem like a non-traditional option – but remember that colleges have not been around forever. You are brave for deciding on a different path; and just like those who choose college, it is the *right* path so long as it is the best path for you.

STUDENT SILHOUETTE: TEGAN

I took part in the ROTC in high school and knew that I wanted to pursue a military career. Rather than pay for college myself, I decided to enlist and join the Air Force. This was one of the best decisions I have ever made.

By joining the Air Force I met some of my best friends. I became an airplane mechanic and felt pride each time I saw a plane flying above me. I also got to travel the world and see places that I could never have afforded to see without joining the military.

After 4 years, I decided to go to college and was accepted to a major private university. Here I studied aerospace engineering and learned more about the airplane parts and processes I worked on as a mechanic in the Air Force. The military paid for my undergraduate degree through the G.I. Bill. I also was received a housing stipend and was reimbursed for my books. Again, there is no way I could have afforded this education without the military's support.

As I finish my degree I am applying to various major airline manufacturers across the industry. I have already been given two job offers before even completing my degree! It is true that the military is not for everyone – but it was absolutely the right choice for me. Thanks to my time in the Air Force I was able to travel, gain a skill, pay for education, and now build a successful career in a field that I love.

STUDENT SILHOUETTE: STEVEN

I knew as soon as I graduated from high school that college wasn't for me. I could not stand the thought of sitting in a classroom listening to a lecture and coming home every day with more homework. My parents, however, thought differently and would not let me live with them if I did not find a job or training.

I did some research and found HVAC technicians (Heating, Ventilation, Air Conditioning) made above minimum wage and had jobs that offered good benefits. Our local technical school offered classes at night, so I decided to work during the day at a car dealership and take HVAC classes at night. I feel like this decision put me ahead of my peers because while they were in classes spending money, I was making money and learning a trade with real-world applications.

Within a year and a half, I left my job at the car dealership and became a full-time HVAC technician. What I like about the job is that there is opportunity for growth – I can advance in the company and make more money as I gain more training and certifications. While my friends are looking for jobs or have to change jobs for more money, my employer pays for my training and offers good benefits. My work schedule does not have a lot of flexibility, but the longer I stay with the company, the more flexibility I will have. The best part is that I never have to do homework again!

REFERENCES

Anders, G. (2017). *You can do anything*. Hachette Book Group.

Angeles, D., & Roberts, B. (2017). Putting your liberal arts degree to work. U.S. Bureau of Labor Statistics. https://www.bls.gov/careeroutlook/2017/article/ liberalarts.htm

ApprenticeshipUSA. (2023). Data and statistics. U.S. Department of Labor. https://www.apprenticeship.gov/data-and-statistics

Arum, R., & Roska, J. (2011). *Academically adrift*. The University of Chicago Press.

Blake, J. (2024). Roadmap of college credit for military experience. *Inside Higher Ed. https://www.insidehighered.com/news/government/state-policy/2024 /04/12/unc-systems-roadmap-college-credit-military-experience?utm_source= Inside+Higher+Ed&utm_campaign=2bb5287be7-DNU_2021_COPY_02 &utm_medium=email&utm_term=0_1fcbc04421-2bb5287be7-238021058&mc _cid=2bb5287be7&mc_eid=0be3e6b198#*

Cuseo, J., Thompson, A., & Campagna, M. (2020). *Thriving in college & beyond: Research based strategies for academic success and personal development* (5th ed.). Kendall Hunt.

Dey, F., & Cruzvergara, C. (2019). Five future directions in university career services. LinkedIn Publication. https://www.linkedin.com/pulse /five-future-directionsuniversity-career-services-faroukdey?articleId =6597727144581877760#comments6597727144581877760&trk=public _profile_article_view

Ezarik, M. (2021). How COVID-19 damaged student success. *Inside Higher Ed.* https://www.insidehighered.com/news/2021/06/21/what-worked -and-what-didn%E2%80%99t-college-students-learning-through-covid -19#:~:text=More%20than%20half%20(52%20percent,somewhat%20 common%20in%20online%20courses

Fain, P. (2020). Report: Resilient job skills in the recession. *Inside Higher Ed.* https://www.insidehighered.com/quicktakes/2020/09/04/report-resilient -job-skillsrecession

Fuller, J., Langer, C., & Sigelman, M. (2022). Skills-based hiring is on the rise. *Harvard Business Review.* https://hbr.org/2022/02/skills-based-hiring -is-on-the-rise

Hanson, M. (2022). College dropout rates. Education Data Initiative. https:// educationdata.org/college-dropout-rates/

Indeed Editorial Team. (2023). 21 skilled trade jobs in-demand. *Indeed.com.* https://www.indeed.com/career-advice/finding-a-job/skilled-trade-jobs -in-demand

Jaschik, S. (2023). Why students opt not to enroll. *Inside Higher Ed.* https:// www.insidehighered.com/news/admissions/2023/06/12/why-students -opt-out-college?utm_source=Inside+Higher+Ed&utm_campaign =8f4624a2fb-DNU_2021_COPY_02&utm_medium=email&utm_term =0_1fcbc04421-8f4624a2fb-237827861&mc_cid=8f4624a2fb&mc_eid =5176a715a3

National Association of Colleges & Employers (NACE). (2021). Career readiness defined. NACE. http://www.naceweb.org/careerreadiness/ competencies/ careerreadiness-defined/

Ruggeri, A. (2019). Why 'worthless' humanities degrees may set you up for life. British Broadcasting Company (BBC). https://www.bbc.com/worklife/article/20190401-why-worthless-humanities-degrees-may-set-you-up-for-life

Seemiller, C., & Grace, M. (2016). *Generation Z goes to college*. Jossey-Bass.

The Burning Glass Institute. (2022). The Emerging degree reset. How the shift to skills-based hiring holds the keys to growing the U.S. workforce at a time of talent shortage. The Burning Glass Institute.

The United States Department of Education (DOE). (2020). Employability skills. U.S. Department of Education, Office of Career, Technical, and Adult Education. http://cte.ed.gov/initiatives/employability-skills-framework

The United States Department of Veterans Affairs (VA). (2023). Positive outcomes of military service. U.S. Department of Veterans Affairs. https://www.va.gov/vetsinworkplace/docs/em_positiveChanges.html

United Services Automobile Association (USAA). (2022). Joining the military after high school. USAA. https://www.usaa.com/inet/wc/advice-military-joining-the-military-after-high-school

Workforce Innovation Technical Assistance Center (WINTAC). (2023). Apprenticeships and customized training. U.S. Department of Education. https://www.wintac.org/topic-areas/apprenticeships-and-customized-training

NAVIGATING THE COLLEGE CHOICE

ABSTRACT

Chapter 4 is the most directive chapter as it relates to the college and university process and environment. This chapter offers realistic advice on how to pursue a college degree – if, of course, this is what a student decides to do after reviewing the data and information presented. College degrees do not always mean employment. The chapter discusses admissions, selecting classes, selecting a major, and advice for engaging on campus. It includes various terms with explanations as well as a Student Silhouettes of a student who chose to go to college.

NO GPS NEEDED

As we begin this chapter, you'll notice specific terms that are related to college and university jargon. These **bold** terms, listed here and in previous chapters are frequently used in higher education and can also be found and defined in Chapter 9. While you navigate your choice about whether or not to attend college, consider the background information related to higher education contained in this chapter. Pay special attention to the section about selecting a major; although college may be the right choice for your career interests, do not confuse your college major with definition of your future career. Remember that a college degree may not always equate to employment. Read on to learn more!

DOI: 10.4324/9781032692258-4

APPLYING

The first step to going to college is applying. You can apply to a college or university through an application that is often found on the college or university website. Generally there are two types of applications that colleges/universities accept. The **common application**, as the name implies, allows you to apply to multiple colleges at the same time through one application. The other type of application is one that is specific to the college/university that you are interested in and is found on the website. It should be noted that applying through the college's specific application is often an indication of your increased attention to that particular college or university. Colleges may prefer or look more favorably upon your application because completing their specific application demonstrates that you took the time to explore their website and specific requirements. It also demonstrates an awareness of whether the specific college or university offers the program that you are pursuing. This intentionality is important when selecting higher education. Completing an application usually takes under an hour, but application processing takes months. Waiting can be one of the most stressful parts of this process for you (and your parents or guardians). But being patient is important – colleges often receive thousands of applicants to select from each enrollment cycle. What students and parents may not know is that although much of the application process is handled online, Admissions processers still ensure all application information is correctly uploaded into their admissions platform/ student database online system. They also confirm various parts of an application so that records do not contain errors or missing components. When applying, be sure to go through the application meticulously – sometimes a simple misspelling in your name or address can cause a delay. Likewise, although you may have requested it, it is crucial to double-check that all of your items, such as high school transcripts and test scores (if applicable) have been submitted. Unfortunately, calling the Admissions Office to check on your status does not decrease your wait time or encourage a faster acceptance decision. Aside from applying, there is nothing more you can do except wait be patient and *check your email regularly* for status updates. Once you receive an admissions decision, then you can move forward.

ADMISSIONS

Admissions decisions vary by institution. They are generally accept-ances (yay!); rejections (sorry!); or waitlists (wait even longer!?); or incomplete applications. In the case of an incomplete application, you will be notified of what is still needed in order for your appli-cation to be processed – but if you ensure everything is submitted sooner, you can save yourself some waiting time. Many institutions no longer require standardized test scores, while some institutions do require them, but may not place as much emphasis on them as in the past. Be sure you are meeting the exact requirements of where you are applying. Some institutions offer **early action** and **early decision**. These are good options if you know for sure that you want to attend a certain college or university – but beware, early options can be binding at some institutions, so be sure to read all of the fine print in your application and acceptance letter.

FINANCIAL AID

Upon acceptance, you must then begin submitting additional required documents. The process varies by institution, but three important documents you should be prepared to submit are the **Free Application for Federal Student Aid (FAFSA)**, **resi-dency documentation**, and your final high school **transcript**, and any previous college transcripts, if applicable.

The FAFSA can be completed online for free through the gov-ernment website (and only the government website), and deter-mines if you are eligible to receive a Pell Grant or other federal financial aid. Even if you do not think you will qualify for aid based on your parents' income – fill it out anyway! Having a FAFSA on file is required for receiving any college or university scholarships, not just federal funds. Many scholarships offered by colleges and universities are need-based, and the FAFSA is often what is used to determine eligibility. Financial aid comes in many forms includ-ing **subsidized loans** and **unsubsidized loans**. Subsidized loans (could be a Stafford loan) are distributed by the government and do not accrue interest while you are enrolled. These loans are only offered to undergraduate students and are based on your finan-cial need as determined by the FAFSA. Unsubsidized loans are not based on financial need and can be administered to undergraduate or graduate students. These loans do not receive any government assistance and begin accruing interest when accepted. Payment on the interest of these types of loans needs to begin shortly after the loan has been disbursed. The Pell Grant, however, is an award that may not require you to have to pay back (yay!). Whether or not a student qualifies for a Pell Grant is based on the expected family contribution (EFC) that is calculated through FAFSA.

It is important to note that loans are different than scholarships and grants. Scholarships are offered by the college/university and are made possible through specific institutional aid or funds raised through private philanthropic giving. Like the Pell Grant, scholarships do not need to be repaid. Students qualify for scholarships by meeting specific standards set by the college or university. Criteria can include financial need (often determined through FAFSA or another standard), or other student attributes such as academic achievement, demographics, intended majors, ancestry, environment, talents, campus involvement, community service, geographic location, and more. Certain scholarships and loans may require that you are a **part-time** student, taking at least 9 credits per semester, or a **full-time student**, taking at least 12 credits per semester. In some cases, certain scholarships require that students must complete a certain number of credit hours during the academic year while earning a certain GPA. Be sure to carefully review any terms associated with a scholarship or loan you receive to ensure that you are meeting the expected requirements to maintain the aid you are receiving. It is also important to know that you may have to "accept" your financial aid package through your college or university website. Financial aid magically appears from the government or institution, but it does not magically apply – you will likely have to accept it and verify that you will be completing classes. Be sure to reach out to your Financial Aid Office or speak with your college's financial aid advisor with questions.

In addition to FAFSA, you will need to have your transcripts on file with the college/university. You can usually request transcripts be sent by asking your high school guidance counselor to email them or by completing a request online through your school website. Your transcripts must be sent directly from your high school if this is your first time attending college, or sent from your previous college or trade school to the college/university in order to be considered "official." Colleges and universities will not accept an "unofficial" transcript when making a final admissions decision. Veterans and active duty military can also submit transcripts of classes you have taken to have them converted to civilian higher education credits. Additionally, veterans and active duty military can also request that their direct experiences be converted to completed college credit through the process of prior learning assessment. As discussed in Chapter 3, veterans and military members have applicable and transferrable skills that are valuable – and it's important that you get credit for your work and service! Institutions may use slightly different processes, but the general process of prior learning assessment is the same. Not all colleges and universities may accept credit earned this way, so be sure to check your institution's website.

Even if you graduated from a high school in the same state as the college, you still need to "declare residency." Different states have different residency requirements – but completing residency documentation is what determines whether you pay in or out-of-state **tuition**. There is a *big* difference in cost; so if you live in a state, be sure to prove it so that you can pay less than your friends from other states. Also, if you are under the age of 24 when applying, your parents/legal guardians must help verify residency by submitting documentation. Along with FAFSA and transcripts, residency is one of the most important documents to prioritize in order to save money and move to your next steps for enrollment.

FERPA AND ADVISING

An optional document for you to complete upon enrollment is the **Federal Education Privacy Act form (FERPA)**. You can think of FERPA as the educational equivalent of the Health Insurance Portability and Accountability Act (HIPAA). Just like a random person cannot call your doctor to find out about your medical history, once you are enrolled in classes, university employees cannot talk to anyone except you regarding your education. This means that if your parent is paying for your college and calls to speak to Financial Aid with a question, they will not be able to share any information about you to your parent unless you have completed the FERPA form or are on the phone too. Similarly, no one can ever find out about your grades, coursework, or schedule without your permission. If you wish to give someone access to this information, you will need to complete a FERPA form with the **Office of the Registrar**. This form allows any individual you wish to call and speak to a university representative on your behalf. Without this on file, a college employee cannot speak to anyone except you.

Every college/university handles enrollment slightly differently, but the institution should provide you with a list of outstanding and necessary items to move forward. Be sure to complete these ASAP and submit everything to the proper office/department! Once everything is complete, and you have received your acceptance packet, there are a couple of additional steps you will need to take to begin your courses. Once you are admitted, you need to secure your seat in your graduating class, which requires that you commit to attending the college/university you selected. This is typically done by paying a deposit (the first of many college payments) and signing up for, or completing an online orientation. Although your Admissions competition is over, you are now in competition for seats in the classes you want to take. The sooner you are fully admitted, the closer you are to registering for classes ... which are generally offered on a first-come-first-serve basis. Once a class is at capacity, that course, that time, with that instructor is no longer available, unless the faculty has allowed a waitlist. Therefore, you must be proactive in completing enrollment steps so that you can complete **orientation** and meet with an **Academic Advisor** (not a counselor like in high school). Do not be afraid to find out who your assigned Advisor is and actively reach out to them. Advisors are important to your college success and are responsible for helping you register for future classes; so it is important to get to know them early in your academic career. Also, Academic Advisors provide the necessary guidance to help you avoid the mistake of taking classes out of sequence or missing **co-requisite** or **pre-requisite** classes.

SELECTING CLASSES

You can select classes during the **add/drop** period of your institution. As a **first-time-in-college (FTIC)** student, your Academic

Advisor generally helps with the initial selection of your courses before, during, or after orientation. But, after that, *you* select your courses during add/drop. You should only consider changing any of your courses at this point if you made a mistake or have a scheduling conflict. Remember that before you started the new semester, your Academic Advisors spent time ensuring your course schedule was designed to keep you on track for your required degree. When you enroll in classes, you have a certain amount of time (generally a week into the semester) to change those classes without having them show up on your final transcript, affect your **GPA**, or impact your college financial aid. In fact, you will be reimbursed for any courses that you change and paid for during the add/drop timeframe. Nevertheless, as soon as add/drop is over (we are talking to the minute) you can no longer change your classes without it impacting your finances, transcript, or GPA. Your course schedule flexibility ends with the end of add/drop. Even though you may not be able to alter your schedule without consequence once add/drop ends, there is still one option for you to leave a class without it impacting your GPA; this is called the **withdrawal period.**

It is vital that you understand that *your GPA is most impacted in your first semester of college.* In fact, if you receive a D or a F in your first semester, you should consider the option of withdrawing so as to avoid starting your college career with a low GPA and possible academic warning that could take you 2–3 future semesters to improve. Withdrawing still holds you fiscally responsible for a course (either charging the full amount or a pro-rated portion); but, instead of receiving a grade that impacts your GPA on your transcript, you will receive a "W," which has no negative consequence on your GPA and thus allows you to complete the course again to earn a satisfactory grade for credit.

*A word of caution: certain scholarships and financial aid packages require that you remain a full-time student. Withdrawing from one or more courses may drop your course load below the minimum number of credits required to maintain your financial aid. Therefore, it is VERY important that prior to withdrawing from any course you speak to your professor, Academic Advisor, or a Financial Aid specialist.

College courses are generally broken down into lower-level coursework with numbers in the 1000s and 2000s (generally taken during your first two years of college) and upper-level coursework in the 3000s and 4000s (generally taken during your third and fourth years of college). Letters in front of the course numbers signify the type of course you are taking. For example, in your first year of college you will likely take a class labeled MAT1033 (or something similar). The prefix MAT stands for a Math class. The numbers 1033 indicate that it is lower-level, such as Intermediate Math (1033).

Every class has a **Course Reference Number (CRN)**. The CRN is the *exact* section of the course that you are taking and it allows the university to tag certain class attributes. It is very common for the same course to have multiple sections/offerings. So, let's say you are taking MAT1033, with a CRN12345. The CRN12345 matches the course to a specific **instructor**, day, time, **semester**, and location of the class. This is important for the Registrar's Office or Office of Records and Registration (the people who approve course schedules), because it allows them to track all of the classes each semester. The CRN usually comes before a course prefix; so when you are selecting classes, you will likely see: CRN12345 MAT1033 with an instructor name, day, time, and location. Be sure to pay attention to this registration information and keep a list of your CRNs so that you ensure you are in the right class.

When selecting a course and considering the chosen instructional modality (how to take the course, such as in-person, online, hybrid, etc.), you must also consider your personal work ethic, time management, motivations, and non-academic commitments. Higher education in the twenty-first century, especially post-pandemic, allows you a plethora of accessibility and flexibility course options. You need to know that the virtual offerings available in higher education are not the same as your virtual high school. Classes can be in-person, asynchronous (online without a meeting day/time), hybrid/blended (partially in-person, partially online), synchronous (Zoom or video learning with certain days/times), or even a mix of multiple modalities. Although the classroom environments have changed, the cost may remain the same or be even higher given university technology fees.

Although online coursework allows for flexibility, this also means adaptability and more study time because the learning is often self-directed. Students are expected to spend a minimum of 3 hours of study per class, per week outside of class time. In addition, you may find that your online classes require more time due to less peer interaction and non-instantaneous professor communication. Although collaboration and learning can happen across all modalities, the age-old axiom remains true: you get out of a course what you put into it. Thus, you must decide where your learning strengths exist and how higher education can help strengthen your learning preferences. You may not instantly love your professor or the way they teach; *however, if you play to your strengths and approach each class with a desire to learn, you will be successful.* For example, if you are a morning person, choose classes earlier in the day. If you have a strict work schedule, consider working on campus instead, as jobs at the college are usually more flexible with class schedules. If you are a self-directed and motivated student who has the time to dedicate to studying, you might consider taking online classes in addition to in-person classes. Also, do not be afraid to reach out to your Academic Advisor for guidance … this is their job to help you be successful!

Finally, when enrolling in classes, it is important to self-identify and reach out to resources given any unique, individual needs. For example, if you have a registered accessibility need such as an individualized education program (IEP/504), you must self-identify with the accessibility office on your campus, such as **Adaptive Services**. Unlike in high school, universities put the onus on students to reach out and take advantage of resources. Note that you must register with your adaptive services office first to determine what accommodations may be offered to assist in your class success. Higher education requires you to self-advocate, so don't be afraid to visit the necessary office to help you with your needs.

SELECTING A MAJOR

Another enrollment consideration is that you may be asked to select a **major** or **degree** program at orientation or before! This often makes an already stressful time worse because the idea of committing to a degree can be daunting … especially when you do not know what you want to study or do not fully understand the options that exist.

Not to fear! A large number of students are accepted to college as "undeclared" majors, while many other students change their majors within their first year of college. In fact, the U.S. Department of

Education reports that about 1/3 of Bachelor's degrees students change their majors once, and 1 in 10 students change majors more than once (DOE, 2017). You should not feel married to the major or degree program that you indicated on your admissions application or Academic Advising form. College administrators may not like to admit it, but many majors can be changed after the first two years of college and still allow you to graduate within four years – but this requires a lot of commitment to classes. As mentioned before, most undergraduate degree programs have common general education requirements or core classes that take approximately 2 years to complete. This is also why Associate's of Arts degrees (A.A.) transfer to colleges and universities. Many students enroll in programs offered at community or state colleges to complete their general education requirements which allows them to transfer directly into their fields of study at a university. By doing so, they pay less in tuition and fees than it would cost to attend a university. They also have had a chance to consider a variety of degrees while completing their A.A., without the perceived pressure of commitment (more on this in Chapter 5).

*A word of caution: once you begin your junior year (third year) of college, if you have not yet decided on a major, or if you decide to change your major, it is very likely that you will be extending your time at the college or university. Many programs have required courses that you must complete in order to satisfy requirements within the degree program. This means more money for more courses. And, certain scholarships may only pay for a certain number of **credit hours**. Therefore, you must be wary of taking too many additional classes outside of your intended major or spending too long exploring different degree programs. Try to select a major by the second semester of your sophomore year (at the latest) to ensure a four-year graduation.

BUT, WHAT DO I MAJOR IN, IF I AM UNSURE WHAT I WANT TO DO?

Although commonly considered, this question is inaccurate for a number of reasons. The first is the misconception that a major must align with a future career. This is not the case. As noted throughout this text, employers are often more concerned about certain skills rather than certain majors. Second, it implies that you must select a major when you are unsure how you want to be employed in the future. For these reasons (and many others), asking this question is rather pointless.

Instead, let's use some career coaching techniques. If you are unsure what you want to major in, rather than ask: "What do I want to do?" it is more meaningful to ask, "What do you *like* to do?" This allows you to consider and then make a list of things that you enjoy doing. The next step is not instantly matching majors; rather, next ask yourself the follow-up questions: "If you close your eyes and envision yourself 5 or 10 years from now, what are you doing? What are you surrounded by? Are you inside? Are you outside? Are there animals? Are there humans? What kind of people are around you?"

Your answers to these questions allow you to narrow down some major and degree options. For example, if you are indoors surrounded by the elderly, health science or health care administration may be a good field to discuss with your Academic Advisor. If you are outdoors surrounded by oceanic animals, marine biology or marine science would seem like a viable option. If you are indoors surrounded by computers, it begs the question: what are you doing with the computers? Are you writing code or developing software or building computers? One requires a four-year degree, the others may not. If you are surrounded by children, consider the age and what you like learning. You can study education, but you can also complete teaching requirements and study a major such as English, history, anthropology, mathematics, biology, chemistry, etc.

This exploratory career coaching technique is valuable when considering what major to choose when enrolling in higher education. However, it needs to be noted (much to the disdain of some of my colleagues and perhaps some parental readers): If you are unsure of what you want to study and are unsure whether or not you want to pursue higher education, then enrolling in *anything* is likely a misguided choice. Rather, research further so that you can begin to determine whether or not attending college at all is your next step.

A college degree may not always equate to employment. For example, recent research from The U.S. Census Bureau in collaboration with the Federal Reserve Bank of New York, presents unemployment rates, expected starting salaries, and mid-range salaries across college majors. According to the data from the U.S. Census Bureau (2023), the majors with the highest unemployment rates include Fine Arts (12.1%), Philosophy (9.1%), Sociology (9%), Family and Consumer Sciences (8.9%), Mass Media (8.4%), Commercial Art and Graphic Design (7.9%), Performing Arts (7.6%), Public Policy and Law (7.4%).

NOW, LET'S BREAK DOWN THE DATA FURTHER …

When we look at the majors with the highest rates of unemployment, they are also the broadest. Fine arts includes artists, musicians, dancers, actors, choreographers, perhaps even writers. Philosophy and sociology are two transferrable majors that can be applied across a variety of career fields. In fact, philosophy majors consistently score in the top percentiles on the Medical College Admission Test (MCAT), Law School Admission Test (LSAT), Graduate Management Admission Test (GMAT), and the Graduate Record Examination (GRE) – often followed by English majors (GMAT, 2011; ETS, 2012; Metcalf, 2021Metm). Consumer services and media are considered some of the fastest-growing fields. So why do they have high unemployment rates? Perhaps we should also ask, why do graduates with an aerospace engineering degree have a higher unemployment rate than those with an anthropology degree (6.6% and 6.4% respectively) when the starting salary is $72,000 compared to $40,000?! (U.S. Census Bureau, 2023). Aerospace engineers would be expected to be in high demand. Speaking of high demand, nursing has the lowest unemployment rate (1.3%) with a starting salary of $55,000, which is one of the lowest in the data (U.S. Census Bureau, 2023). Obviously demand does not always match pay.

Majors and salaries vary while economic trends and employment rates are constantly in flux. Ultimately the data is useful for offering a broad concept of what majors may automatically help in getting jobs and high wages based on supply and demand. But, beware of selecting a major *only* based on the data. Certain majors are applicable across fields and provide you with transferrable skills. Selecting a major based solely on the job market could leave you in a job you may not enjoy at the mercy of an ever-changing economy.

Overall, if business leaders do not believe students are gaining necessary skills in higher education, it may be because the students themselves (*you*) are also unaware of your skill development and degree transferability. Many students attend college seeking degrees with titles that define future careers (i.e., nursing = nurse, education = teacher, accounting = accountant). This is an easy solution to the anxiety-provoking question asked of so many people your age: "What are you going to do with that degree?" Unfortunately, students are often unsure which career opportunities align with degrees outside of those that manifest corresponding titles. However, the critical thinking, logic, communication/rhetoric, and problem-solving skills learned in less-defined courses can be easily applied to a variety of career fields and employment opportunities. Therefore, be sure that you research the majors and degrees that you want to pursue in order to identify whether or not you will gain the skills employers are seeking. Also, do not forget to consider whether or not you enjoy the coursework and skills (or perhaps just enjoy the ability to avoid explaining why you are going to do with your future).

Colleges and universities are not the doors to open all job opportunities. Certain vocations require credentials in the form of certificates and training rather than degrees. Other pathways to careers can be achieved through **internships** or **apprenticeships** and allow for career and salary progression based on years on the job and level of experience gained (these are further discussed in Chapters 3 and 9). Unfortunately, colleges and universities often make the assumption that "one-size-fits-all" for different majors and degrees. Therefore, it is incumbent upon you (and your parents if applicable) to research many opportunities related to your personal interests. And, if at the end of the day you are still unsure and overly stressed about what major or career to pursue, you can declare "undecided" as your major or perhaps save time and resources by allowing a year or two of voluntary vocational exploration and employment to narrow down your interests. Do not overlook your unique skills and talents – these are often good guides to where your interest and success can lie in your career.

*Another note of caution: a year or two of vocational exploration is not to be confused with the term "gap year," often used to refer to time taken after high school before moving to higher education.

Fewer students are attending college directly out of high school than in the past (Knox, 2023). If you are not seeking higher education post-graduation, you should be seeking employment, self-autonomy, and financial independence. Some students may need some extra time to adapt to adulthood. Nevertheless, many therapists will affirm that exposure is an answer to anxiety (Johnson & Ridley, 2004), and exposing yourself to different major and career options will help reduce your anxiety and allow for direction and narrowing of your future goals. So, start trying jobs and learn what you like. College is not for everyone, but learning should be a lifelong pursuit.

ENGAGING ON CAMPUS

The first year of college can be a challenging adjustment for any student. Many first-time-in-college students experience anxiety, loneliness, and low self-esteem in their freshman year (So & Fiori, 2022). In fact, college freshman account for almost 27% of dropout rate data within their first 12 months! This is unfortunately especially true of first-generation and minority students (Potochnick & Perreira, 2010).

Do not let this data define you!

One of the best ways for you to be successful early on in your academic career is to take advantage of all of the tools and resources that the college or university offers – as soon as possible! College education comes with a cost, and much of the student fees you are paying are dedicated to academic support services and well-being initiatives such as tutoring, counseling, career coaching, mental health resources, food pantries, student organizations, events, and activities. If you are paying for it anyway in your student fees, you may as well use it!

While you are socializing on campus, some of the most important people to get to know are your college professors. Professors are far more likely to offer assistance, share resources, and be understanding when they get to know you on a personal level and see you active in their class. This means that you should ask questions and visit them during their **office hours**. Office hours are required of **faculty** and are the perfect time for you to stop in to ask questions, review your grades, or even discuss possible career options associated with their field of study. Getting to know your professors will help you on a personal and academic level. Visiting your professor during their office hours shows them that you cared enough to seek out their guidance – and they appreciate this! What's more, research shows that students who are mentored in college demonstrate better GPAs, lower class failure rates, and higher persistence and retention rates (Salinitri, 2005). Therefore, do not be afraid to ask questions or get to know individuals with experiences on campus who can help mentor you through the process...and use this book to mentor you too!

Being engaged on campus is multifaceted. You can (and should) visit the college/university academic support centers for free tutoring and coaching. All students can take part in fun activities such as food trucks, parties, free swag events, etc. You can also "rush" fraternities or sororities (Greek life) as a means of social interaction. However, there are also leadership activities and ways to engage on campus that can help your résumé. For example, by taking on a leadership position such as peer mentor, student coach, or service-learner/volunteer, you are expanding your college network and gaining employment skills. Do not underestimate the importance of college connections and be sure to introduce yourself to a peer in each course so that you have someone to reach out to if you miss a class. Developing an academic support network will help you succeed further!

Research from the Center for the Study of Student Life at Ohio State University (OSU) shows that student involvement on campus is linked to brain development, psychological well-being, academic performance, multicultural awareness, and leadership skills (OSU, 2023). In fact, employers preferred students who were involved in campus life (OSU, 2020). How much did employers care about student involvement? According to the data, highly involved students were considered 18% more career-ready (OSU, 2020), and were three times more likely to be considered for employment (OSU, 2023).

WHAT DOES ALL OF THIS MEAN FOR YOU?

Just like anything else, you get out of college what you put into it. If you are a "car to class" student who is only on campus during class time, you will be missing out on unique opportunities and experiences that are unique to the university environment. Do not overextend yourself at the expense of your academics; but make the most of your time on campus and take advantage of resources for your personal, academic, and career success.

In order to maximize your personal potential and opportunities in college, what remains crucial is that you seek future employment skills (not necessarily just a degree) that can be transferred to multiple jobs and workplaces. Research confirms that graduates entering the current workforce are likely to change careers and jobs multiple times (National Academy of Sciences, 2018). In fact, some data projects that recent graduates will change careers up to 11 times before the age of 50 (Gallup & Bates, 2019; Pasquerella, 2019). It is for this reason that higher education needs to remain committed to preparing its students for a variety of occupations. The National Academy of Sciences (2018) notes:

> Faculty and administrators, who are concerned that an education focused on a single discipline will not best prepare graduates for the challenges and opportunities presented by work, life, and citizenship in the 21st century, are advocating for an approach to education that moves beyond the general education requirements found at almost all institutions. (p. x)

You must approach your academic pursuits with a broad focus on interdisciplinary skills across degrees, even though the workforce is often dictated by projected job growth. Over the next 9 years, the U.S. Bureau of Labor Statistics (2020) projects an 8% growth in STEM jobs (Science, Technology, Engineering, Mathematics). However, the fastest-growing occupation for 2020–2030 is wind turbine service technician (BLS, 2023), which requires skills, training, and certifications rather than a specific major or degree. As even the dropout billionaires can attest, a university degree does not always equate to necessary employment skills; thus, college may not be the best pathway to your desired career. Choosing college is a good choice so long as it is the *right* choice for your future goals. Keep reading to learn more about how to best inform your college choice.

The figure below offers a glimpse of how long you can plan to spend in higher education depending on which degree you pursue. Your college choices and how many classes you take each semester also impact your time in college. The degrees are explained in the forthcoming chapters and the acronyms can be found in Chapter 9.

~8-10 years	• Doctoral degrees such as Ph.D., M.D., D.V.M
~6 years	• Master's degrees such as M.A., M.S., M.F.A, M.B.A.
~4 years	• Bachelor's degrees such as B.A., B.S., B.S.A.
~2 years	• Associate's degrees such as A.A. or A.S. • Certificate or Industry credential

STUDENT SILHOUETTE: JESSI

I went directly from high school to a large public university. Although I didn't know what to study at first, I decided to major in biology because it felt broad enough to allow me to get a job after graduation. Plus, I always enjoyed science classes and thought it would be more fun to work in a lab instead of writing lots of long papers.

After adjusting to college life and classes, I decided to get involved. I enjoyed the orientation when I toured the campus with my family and thought it would be fun to participate. So, I applied, interviewed, and was accepted. For the summer of my sophomore year, I was an Orientation Leader. I met every incoming student and worked closely with a team of my peers. Part of our job was to learn about the campus resources, so I found out about a ton of opportunities on campus. This helped me get more connected and involved. It was a blast getting to know the other leaders. We would work together all day and then hang out after the orientations. They became my first real friends on campus.

Being an Orientation Leader definitely pushed me out of my comfort zone and let me meet a lot of new people. I never thought I could talk to a room of 100 students. Although it was fun, I decided not to do it again after my sophomore year because of the time commitment. Instead, I worked off-campus as a barista and became a peer tutor. Balancing these jobs was easy because working on campus really helped me manage my time and the barista job was part-time on the weekends near campus where my friends would visit.

While tutoring other students, I realized that the classes I enjoyed talking about most often were environmentally focused. I spoke to my Advisor and switched my major to environmental studies. Since most of my biology classes overlapped, I didn't lose any time toward graduation. Part of my job as an Orientation Leader was to tell students to get involved and I felt like a hypocrite not being active on campus. So, I joined the Environmental Services Club and began volunteering with friends at the garden on campus. I also spoke to one of my professors about job opportunities working with plants. He recommended that I contact a local organization that had a nature walk and garden.

I quit my peer tutor job on campus, increased my hours as a barista, and began volunteering at the garden a few days a week. I got to work in the field and apply what I was learning in my classes. I graduated in 4 years and the garden offered me a full-time job, where I work today. I love being surrounded by nature and am looking into graduate programs so that I can do research on environmental sustainability practices and start my own garden and farm.

One piece of advice I would offer to any student is "Get involved!" If I hadn't pushed myself out of my comfort zone and become an Orientation Leader, I probably never would have felt confident enough to join a campus club. Joining that club led to new friends and volunteering. Now I have a full-time job and am thinking of going to graduate school. If you go to college, get involved!

STUDENT SILHOUETTE: TORIN

When I graduated from high school I received an athletic scholarship to a small, private, liberal arts college not far from my home. In the summer of my sophomore year, my parents decided to relocate and I wanted to be close to them, so I applied to a large, public university not far from their new home.

Taking classes at the private college was very different from the public one. Classes were bigger and I felt like it was harder to find resources at the new school. I also had to be a "walk-on" for the sports team and decided to play club intramural instead. Rather than having someone tell me where to go or what to do, I had to ask my classmates. Once I found the resources like tutoring, the fitness center, advising, etc., it was great – but I don't know if I would have had gotten the help and found things if I had never asked.

I loved how diverse the university was and enjoyed going to the football games and doing things that weren't offered at the private college. The private college had a strong academic focus, but it was expensive and would have required the same amount of time to graduate, even though I was in a specialized program. The public university made me feel comfortable and allowed me to take classes while working and playing my sport for fun. I thought I had to go to the small private school because of my degree – but when I transferred, the university had a similar degree that led me to the same career path. Although it had a different title, my Advisor explained that I could still go into the same field. Before transferring, I didn't know that degrees could have different names but still allow you to get the same job or go into the same area of work. In my case, I changed to a broader major but took courses that focused on the area of work I am in.

One piece of advice I suggest is to consider all of your options when applying to college. The diversity and flexibility of the larger university was a better fit for me. I am also glad that I transferred because in my case, I expanded my degree options which broadened my career options. Now that I've received my Bachelor degree, I have decided to continue on to get my Master's degree. My wife and I are both proud graduates who still go to as many football games as we can.

REFERENCES

Educational Testing Service (ETS). (2012). GRE guide to the use of scores. Educational Testing Service. https://www.ets.org/s/gre/pdf/gre_guide_table4.pdf

Gallup & Bates. (2019). Forging pathways to purposeful work. The role of higher education. Gallup.

Graduate Management Admission Council (GMAT). (2011). Profile of GMAT candidates. Graduate Management Admission Council. http://www.gmac.com/market-intelligence-and-reseaerch/research-library/gmat-test-taker-data.aspx

Johnson, W. B., & Ridley, C. R. (2004). *The elements of mentoring.* Palgrave Macmillan.

Knox, L. (2023). After a decade of growth, degree earners decline. *Inside Higher Ed.* https://www.insidehighered.com/news/2023/03/17/undergrad-degree-completion-falls-first-time-decade?utm_source=Inside+Higher+Ed&utm_campaign=5ddd470a95-DNU_2021_COPY_02&utm_medium=email&utm_term=0_1fcbc04421-5ddd470a95-237308953&mc_cid=5ddd470a95&mc_eid=1cf83c82c9

Metcalf, T. (2021). Philosophy majors & high standardized test scores: Not just correlation. *Daily Nous.* https://dailynous.com/2021/07/14/philosophy-majors-high-standardized-test-scores/

Pasquerella, L. (2019). Yes, employers do value liberal arts degrees. *Harvard Business Review.* https://hbr.org/2019/09/yes-employers-do-value-liberal-arts-degrees

Potochnick, S., & Perreira, K. (2010). Depression and anxiety among first-generation immigrant Latino youth: Key correlates and implications for future research. *The Journal of Nervous and Mental Disease, 198*(7), 470–477. https://doi.org/10.1097/NMD.0b013e3181e4ce24

Salinitri, G. (2005). The effects of formal mentoring on the retention rates for first-year, low achieving students. *Canadian Journal of Education*, *28*(4), 873–853. https:// 10.2307/4126458

So, C., & Fiori, K. (2021). Attachment anxiety and loneliness during the first-year of college: Self-esteem and social support as mediators. *Personality and Individual Differences*, *187*. https://doi.org/10.1016/j.paid.2021.111405

The National Academy of Sciences. (2018). *The integration of the humanities and arts with sciences, engineering, and medicine in higher education: Branches from the same tree.* The National Academies Press. https://doi.org/10.17226/24988

The Ohio State University Center for the Study of Student Life. (2020). Involvement, leadership and student outcomes at graduation. The Ohio State University. https://cssl.osu.edu/research-projects/involvement-study

The Ohio State University Center for the Study of Student Life. (2023). Involvement in college matters. The Ohio State University. https://cssl.osu .edu/research-projects/involvement-study

The United States Bureau of Labor Statistics. (2020). Occupational outlook handbook. United States Bureau of Labor. https://www.bls.gov/ooh/

The United States Bureau of Labor Statistics. (2022). Occupational employment projections to 2022. U.S. Bureau of Labor Statistics. https://www.bls.gov/opub/mlr/2013/article/occupational-employment -projections-to2022.htm#:~:text=From%202012%20to%202022%2C %20the,occupations%20and%20decline%20in%20others

The United States Bureau of Labor Statistics. (2023). Fastest growing occupations. United States Bureau of Labor. https://www.bls.gov/ooh/ fastest-growing.htm

The United States Department of Education (DOE). (2017). Data point: Beginning college students who change their majors within 3 years of enrollment. U.S. DOE. https://nces.ed.gov/pubs2018/2018434.pdf

IS AN ASSOCIATE DEGREE RIGHT FOR ME?

ABSTRACT

Chapter 5 focuses mainly on two-year institution information associated with community/state colleges and Associate's degrees. It provides data and examples of when an Associate degree may be a good choice for a student's academic and career goals. Additionally, this chapter contains a graphic of the different Associate's degrees and two Student Silhouettes about students who made this college choice.

WHAT EVEN IS AN ASSOCIATE DEGREE?

The terms **college** and **university** are often used interchangeably. However, they are different in their meanings. A college is a higher education institution that offers undergraduate degrees (four-year Bachelor's degrees) in various disciplines. It may be **public** (non-profit), **private** non-profit, or private **for-profit**. A university is a higher education institution that offers undergraduate degrees (four-year Bachelor's degrees) and graduate degrees (graduate degrees vary in year requirements). Just like a college, universities can be public, private, or for-profit. Some universities are **land grant institutions**, which offer courses in agriculture and farming. There are also types of university that have special Federal designation based on their mission in serving a specific population of students. **Historical Black Colleges and Universities (HBCUs)** predominantly serve African Americans, while **Hispanic Serving Institutions (HSIs)** predominantly serve students of Hispanic or

DOI: 10.4324/9781032692258-5

Latin origins. Two-year colleges most often offer what are known as Associate's degrees.

The term "**Associate degree**" goes back to the University of Oxford in England. As one of the first universities, Oxford originally used this term to certify its students who completed a required number of classes (Acland, 1858). Nowadays, and especially in Western education, the term is generally applied to a two-year degree. Associate's degrees are often obtained from **community or state colleges** that are **accredited** (educationally qualified). This degree is meant to be one that can be obtained within two years and can be pursued alongside industry certifications. In fact, many community/state colleges are focused on career and technical education, meaning that their coursework (**curriculum**) is linked directly to a career such as an aviation technician or a dental hygienist.

Associate's degrees can be "**Associate of Arts (A.A.)**" or "**Associate of Science (A.S.)**." An Associate of Arts degree is a two-year degree that is gained once you finish your required **general or core education** coursework. "Arts" is a broad term that means that you completed the necessary college **credits** in order to earn your degree. An Associate of Science degree is also a broad term that means that you completed the necessary college credits in order to earn your degree; however, an A.S. degree is generally designed to allow you to go directly into the workforce with specific skills following graduation. It is important to note that although both of these degrees are termed "two-year" degrees, the amount of time it will take you to complete them depends on how many credits you take per semester and what program you choose. In order to actually complete your degree and graduate in two years, you will likely have to take a certain number of credits per semester, which may include summer. The main difference in whether you want to obtain an A.A. or A.S. lies in your future goals:

If you want to go to a university and study *any* major (English, art, engineering, biology, business, etc.) after your first two years in college, you will most likely need an A.A. degree.

If you want to go directly into the workforce following your first two years of college and begin a career with your skills, you will most likely need an A.S. degree. See the graphic below.

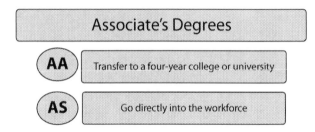

This can be confusing, particularly if you want to go into a STEM (science, technology, engineering, mathematics) field. Students often say, "I don't want to get an arts degree, I want to get a science degree." Despite the confusing terminology, if you want to study ANY degree at a future college or university, you will likely need an A.A. to avoid taking additional classes when you transfer to a four-year institution after completing your two-year degree.

Why? Remember that an Associate degree is meant to certify that you completed the necessary coursework and credits to complete your degree. The necessary coursework within the first two years of college is meant to be a broad exposure to a variety of **disciplines** (fields of study). Most Associate's degrees allow you to complete your necessary general education requirement courses so that you can then transfer or start your career. If you pursue an A.S. degree, you will likely take classes that are more aligned with a professional technical field, so you will have some general education coursework and some skills-based coursework. The skills-based classes take the place of other courses, so you may not complete the same general education courses as students pursuing their A.A. degree. General education courses are required at community/state colleges AND universities based on state accreditation; so if you get an A.S. degree and then transfer to a university, you will still start as a junior (so long as you completed an Associate degree), but you will likely have to take additional general education courses before beginning upper-level classes in your academic program or major.

VOCATIONAL ASSOCIATE'S DEGREES

Some vocational colleges, two-year colleges, or technical schools may offer unique Associate's degrees. These degrees may be

Associate of Occupational Studies (A.O.S.) or **Associate of Applied Science (A.A.S.)**. These degrees are specific to the college program and are skills-based to provide you with the necessary training to go directly into the workforce. Unlike the more common A.S. and A.A. degrees, A.O.S. and A.A.S. degrees are not designed to include general education courses in a typical college setting. Instead, these are skills-based and workplace-driven for students who know exactly what industry they want to pursue. These are less commonly offered degrees, so be sure to research the program thoroughly to ensure it matches your specific career goals.

WHY WOULD YOU GET AN ASSOCIATE DEGREE?

Associate's degrees are great for a number of reasons: 1.) They allow you to get a "jump start" on college in a smaller, often friendlier environment. 2.) Many students **dual enroll** (take college-level classes while still in high school) at community/state colleges that offer Associate's degrees, so that they become familiar with the college campus culture. 3.) If you are the first in your family to attend college (**first-generation**), community/state colleges often require college classes that help reinforce college-level skills. These prove very beneficial to students who need to know more about college life. 4.) Community/state colleges generally offer *the same* lower-level, general education courses as public universities *at a lower price* … so you are taking college classes and paying less than your peers at universities … plus these courses usually transfer easily to a public university. 5.) Faculty at community/state colleges sometimes teach at a university too, so taking lower-level classes with the same faculty in a smaller class size is a great introduction to college life.

In addition, research has shown that although more jobs require higher degrees than in the past, someone with an Associate degree can earn more than someone with a Bachelor degree depending on the field of study (Burke, 2020). For example, the majority of dental hygienists (who make a median annual salary of over $78,000!) have a top education level of an Associate degree (Career Coach, 2023). Also, Associate's degrees on average bring much higher wages than certificates or high school diplomas (Capsee, 2017). This means that you can pay less for your degree and earn more!

One of the most appealing elements of Associate's degrees earned at community colleges is that you can balance your coursework with your work. More than half (58%) of students at community colleges between the ages of 18–24 work in addition to taking their classes (Weissman, 2023). In comparison to university students, community college students are 10% more likely to be over the age of 21 (43%) and are 38% more likely to attend part-time (68%) when compared to university students (Schanzenbach et al., 2023).

Post-pandemic, first-time Associate's degrees graduates fell 7.6%, which is more than any other degree type (NSCRC, 2023). Enrollment among community college students declined by 6% in the year following the minimum wage increase and has remained low (NSCRC, 2022; Schanzenbach et al., 2023). With over 55% total of state/community college students working, these students are more affected by minimum wage changes, which could be why community colleges have a lower persistence rate (fewer students completing degrees) than universities (NSCRC, 2022; Schanzenbach et al., 2023). An average of 34% of Associate's degrees students complete their program within 3 years, which is a year longer than expected (Schanzenbach et al., 2023). It becomes clear, then, that students who pursue Associate's degrees are paying for them with the wages they are earning and are often willing to sacrifice the degree or the amount of time it takes to earn it in order to earn more money.

For this reason, when pursuing an Associate degree, it is especially important to consider your long-term goals and how your college plans support them. Perhaps most valuable with Associate's degrees is that by the time you complete an A.A. or A.S., you are often better equipped to decide whether or not to continue in higher education or go directly into the workforce. Now you know what college-level coursework is like, and whether or not it is for you. You can remain at the community or state college to complete an A.A. or A.S. degree; you can be a **transient** student and remain enrolled at a state college but take courses at a university or another college for certain classes; or in some cases, you can even remain at a community or state college to complete a four-year Bachelor degree. The next chapter discusses what a Bachelor's degree is, and why you may want to pursue one.

STUDENT SILHOUETTE: THANG

In high school my guidance counselor suggested that I dual enroll. I didn't know what this meant at first, but realized that if I took college classes while in high school, I wouldn't have to pay for them in college. Being on a college campus as a high school student was intimidating at first. But I quickly realized that there were a lot of people from a lot of different backgrounds and ages on campus with me.

I took one English class and one math class to get ahead. The course-work was not too different than high school – but the teaching was. I had to study a lot more outside of class time because, unlike high school, there were things I was expected to know from the readings when I went to class. Also, the professors had strict deadlines and expected me to be able to know what was due by checking online.

I got an A and a B in my first two classes and have decided to stay at the community college to complete my A.A. The good thing about dual enrollment was that I am now familiar with the campus, professors, and resources. Plus, I am saving a lot of money that my friends are not because college is more affordable, and I can finish high school and work while taking classes. Also, I have found the campus to be comfortable and the staff to be friendly and willing to help other students like me. I am not sure what I want to do when I graduate; but for now, I am happy finishing my A.A. ahead of my friends because I dual enrolled.

Based on my experience, I would recommend dual enrolling and attending a state or community college. I have found the environment to be friendly and helpful. It has also been nice to know that I can be working toward my degree while working. While my friends have been super stressed about deciding on their universities and future careers, I have been pursuing my A.A. I will eventually decide what the future holds for me, but for now will keep working, saving money, and taking classes while I figure it out.

STUDENT SILHOUETTE: BEN

My educational experience is a story to tell. I have had successes, failures, and there have been challenges along the way. Both of my parents went to college and earned Bachelor's degrees. My grandfather has a Doctorate degree. From the time I was in elementary school my parents were asking me where I wanted to go to college. In my senior year of high school, I slacked off. My GPA, SAT/ACT scores were not as good as they could have been. So although I wanted to go to the same university as my parents, my grades did not allow me to do so. I applied to three different universities and didn't get accepted into any. I decided to apply to the community college in our area instead. Shortly after my acceptance, I received an invitation to a leadership retreat at the college. After much convincing from my parents and grandparents, I went to the retreat and became a part of a whole new world that I never anticipated. The retreat taught me about leadership, college skills, and more importantly, it gave me the confidence I needed to start college. It was scary to go somewhere that I didn't know anyone – but I'm glad I went because I met a lot of people.

My major is business so that I can work with my dad in his company. But right now, I'm actually working on developing an app. Going to college at the community college level allows me to work on my app while taking classes and learning from my dad. Even though I did not end up at the same university as my parents, I think this college has been better for me personally. To me, it's the best of both worlds … work and study.

One piece of advice I would offer to other students is to try to decide what type of college experience is best for you. By choosing a community college and majoring in business, I can focus on what I want rather than having to go through four years at a different school where I may not be as successful.

REFERENCES

Acland, T. (1858). *Some account of the origin and objects of the new Oxford examinations for the title of associate in arts, and certificates for the year 1858.* J. Ridgway. https://archive.org/details/someaccountofori00acla/page/n37/mode/2up

Burke, L. (2020). Certificates and associate degrees can outearn bachelor's. *Inside Higher Ed.* https://www.insidehighered.com/quicktakes/2020/01/29/certificates-and-associate-degrees-can-outearn-bachelor%E2%80%99s

Career Coach. (2023). Career coach. Emsi. www.fsw.emsicc.com

Center for Analysis of Postsecondary Education and Employment (Capsee). (2017). Degrees lead on wages. *Inside Higher Ed.* https://www.insidehighered.com/news/2017/03/29/wages-earnings-increase-significantly-associate-degree-holders

National Student Clearinghouse Research Center (NSCRC). (2022). More than 39 million Americans have some college, no credential, according to new research. National Student Clearinghouse. https://www.studentclearinghouse.org/more-than-39-million-americans-have-some-college-no-credential-according-to-new-research/

National Student Clearinghouse Research Center (NSCRC). (2023). Undergraduate degree earners. Academic year 2021–2022. National Student Clearinghouse. https://nscresearchcenter.org/undergraduate-degree-earners/

Schanzanbach, D. W., Turner, J. A., & Turner, S. (2023). Raising state minimum wages, lowering community college enrollment. National Bureau of Economic Research. http://www.nber.org/papers/w31540

Weissman, S. (2023). Minimum wage gains, community college enrollment losses. *Inside Higher Ed.* https://www.insidehighered.com/news/institutions/community-colleges/2023/08/09/enrollment-drops-two-year-colleges-after-minimum?utm_source=Inside+Higher+Ed&utm_campaign=81a5bd119d-DNU_2021_COPY_02&utm_medium=email&utm_term=0_1fcbc04421-81a5bd119d-237827861&mc_cid=81a5bd119d&mc_eid=5176a715a3#

6

IS A BACHELOR DEGREE
RIGHT FOR ME?

ABSTRACT

This chapter provides background on different Bachelor's degrees as well as the common terms associated with this undergraduate degree. Chapter 6 provides data context on how Bachelor's degrees are viewed in the workforce and why a student may want to pursue this degree. Additionally, this chapter includes a Student Silhouette of an architectural engineer who received his Bachelor degree to build skyscrapers, and a student who chose to return to community college to complete her Bachelor degree.

WHAT EVEN IS A BACHELOR DEGREE?

The term "**Bachelor Degree**" was used in early education to distinguish lower-level, **undergraduate** degrees from the Master's and doctoral qualifications of the time. In order to earn a Bachelor degree, individuals had to pass a Baccalaureate exam (Costa, 2022). This is why a Bachelor degree is often interchangeably referred to as a **Baccalaureate degree**.

Bachelor's degrees are generally four-year degrees. Like with an Associate degree, depending on how many classes you take in a **semester**, it may take you longer to earn your degree; however, the average number of required credits or hours is likely 120 with an associated timeframe of about four years, including summer semester courses. You can earn a **Bachelor of Arts (B.A.)** or a

DOI: 10.4324/9781032692258-6

Bachelor of Science (B.S.) degree. Less common but also possible, is a **Bachelor of Science and Arts degree (B.S.A)**.

Associate degree credits can count toward Bachelor degree credits because like "Associate," Bachelor is also a broad term that means you completed the necessary college credits in order to earn your degree. However, unlike Associate's degrees, the denotation of Arts or Sciences is related to what you choose to study rather than whether or not you intend to go directly into the workforce. For example, if you choose a **humanities** degree such as history, art, anthropology, English, education, communications, etc., you will receive a Bachelor of Arts. Likewise, if you study biology, engineering, business, mathematics, chemistry, physics, nursing, etc., you will earn a Bachelor of Science degree. Both degrees are considered "Bachelor's" and hold the same value at the university and in the workforce.

Bachelor's degrees are given (or conferred) by a college or university that is accredited. You will notice that Bachelor's degrees are most often associated with a **university** rather than a community or state college. This is because universities offer **graduate degrees** as well, and in order to be considered "a university," the institution must also be accredited with advanced degrees.

When you receive your **diploma**, it will say "Bachelor of Science" or "Bachelor of Arts" and then list the major you studied. Diplomas do not include any **minors** or additional information, though you can study a minor or a **concentration** if there is an area in which you are additionally interested in. For example, if you are an environmental studies major who is very interested in sustainability practices, you may work with your Academic Advisor or faculty members to concentrate on sustainability classes. If there are enough classes offered at your institution and it is approved based on the curriculum, you may major in environmental studies and concentrate on sustainability. Remember, however, that only your major will be included on your diploma. Your concentration will be noted in your transcripts. Likewise, if you are a history major who is interested in teaching, you might consider minoring in secondary education. Your history degree will be within one college (likely the College of Arts and Sciences or /Humanities) and your minor will be within another college (the College of Education).

You will complete a certain number of course credits within the College of Education to qualify as a minor. As before, only the major will be noted on your diploma; the minor will be evident on your transcripts. In addition to minors and concentrations, you can also add to your education with microcredentials. See Chapter 8 for more information.

⋆A note of clarity here. In case you hadn't noticed, higher education has colleges that exist within a university. As if it wasn't confusing enough! At four-year universities, your major is within your degree program. Your degree is within a college. Your college is within a university. Put another way, let's say you are studying business. Your major would be within the field of business, likely something such as business administration or accounting. Your major is within your degree program (Bachelor) in the College of Business. The College of Business is one of the university colleges. It is for reasons like *this* that I have written this book and hope it helps to clarify for you.

The Office of the Registrar, or Records and Registration, is the campus office that determines whether or not you qualify for your degree and graduation. Know that you will need to apply to graduate in advance of a certain deadline so that the office can confirm that you have completed all necessary course requirements and are on track to graduate. Be sure to constantly check your email and college website for graduation due dates.

WHY WOULD YOU GET A BACHELOR DEGREE?

Bachelor's degrees can be considered synonymous with undergraduate degrees, and are often a gateway for academic and personal advancement. Although it is the most common postsecondary degree conferred in the U.S., only 52.8 million Americans hold this degree (U.S. Census Bureau, 2022). Post-pandemic, 2.5% fewer students completed Bachelor's degrees following their Associate's degrees, and for the first time in a decade, 2.4% fewer students earned Bachelor's degrees overall (NSCRC, 2023). This means that if you pursue a Bachelor degree, you will set yourself apart from others in the workforce and likely begin a career at a higher wage than those without a four-year degree, especially given the decline.

Additionally, since 87% of students in four-year universities receive some form of financial aid, they may be less impacted by economic wage changes (NCES, 2023).

Despite the benefits, since the pandemic, college enrollments have continued to decline (Jaschik, 2023). Some of the main reasons students have chosen not to attend college include mental health, feelings of inadequate academic preparation, and delayed research in college opportunities (Jaschik, 2023). It is important to take care of yourself and educate yourself on your academic and career options. Research indicates that the more you gain career knowledge and increase occupational information self-efficacy (a belief in your ability to perform well in a given task) the more career action steps you are likely to take (Cordova, 2022). In other words, self-efficacy gained from informed knowledge can inspire you to take more steps toward your career goals, which can increase your confidence in your choices. However, without proper guidance and an understanding of the application and transferability of your degrees or skills, you can have a difficult time finding initial employment. Therefore, when deciding on a four-year degree, you should consider your personal strengths and the topics/activities you enjoy so that you can develop and build skills around those areas.

Choosing to go directly to college may be the right decision for you based on your current and future goals. You can also begin your career while pursuing your four-year degree. Data shows that only 46% of students between the ages of 18 to 24 work while attending a four-year institution, but they often work at higher wages (Schanzanbach et al., 2023). If you do choose to pursue a degree alongside your work, it is important to remember that colleges and universities are not paradigms for the business world and everyone's future careers. From the manner of dress, the expectation of debate and discourse, to the opportunities and variance of opinions, campuses are microcosms of communities that are not often replicated off campus. College students are treated as adults who are autonomous, but the responsibility is on *you* to make good choices and take advantage of the resources.

For better or for worse, universities indulge and shelter students in ways that will not be replicated in their current or future careers. This is why so many students think so fondly of their college experiences – it is a time of life when you are allowed to be vocal and explore opportunities without the same costs and consequences as when you are no longer reliant on grades to determine self-worth and advancement. Outside of university settings, grades become pay scales, professors are now bosses, and opportunities are limited with costs. There is less allowance for mistakes and ignorance because teaching or training may not be a common practice at your workplace. This can be a hard adjustment if your schedule allows you to attend every "Thirsty Thursday" because you have no classes on Friday.

Although this may sound harsh or judgmental – it is not. Rather, it is an attempt to help you understand that *despite what professors may tell you, and what you may think, doing well academically does not indicate employability.*

You may be wondering: "Isn't it the college's job to recruit me and then help me get a job?" Although it may seem as though colleges are doing students a disservice, the reality is that the responsibility is on *you* to research college and career options to determine the best choices for you. Just like you decide what you want to study, how many classes you want to take, how long you want to be in college – you also decide whether or not to build career skills. It is true that colleges and universities offer platforms for professional learning and experiences – but *you* must choose to take advantage of them and actively apply your learning to your life and workplace. Colleges and universities often provide co-curricular (alongside academic) programs to help you develop your career and professional skills that may not be taught in your classes. Take advantage of the career development services offices on your campus. Participate in job fairs, networking events, interview workshops, **externships**, and **internships**. Job fairs allow you to meet with many employers and share your résumé with many hiring employers. Networking events help you learn to interact with professionals in your chosen career or industry. Interview workshops teach you the necessary communication skills and interview strategies. Externships are unpaid job shadowing experiences, and internships are working with an employer through a paid or unpaid opportunity to learn the workplace environment and gain necessary skills. Thus, in order to get the most out of your college experience and get employed, take active steps to learn from career professionals alongside your professors while getting your degree.

STUDENT SILHOUETTE: FRANCIS

From the time I was a child living in South America, I knew I wanted to be an architectural engineer. My family was supportive, but sometimes thought I was crazy. My opportunity was nothing like what they experienced growing up. My parents did not have the chance to attend college like I did, and they were nervous about me going abroad, but also wanted what was best for me. I researched some of the best colleges in the U.S. and applied. I wanted a university that was competitive, but would also allow me to have a good time while abroad and engage in the "American college" experience.

When I got accepted to my first choice, I was thrilled. I engaged with the International Services office and knew I would need to keep my grades up in order to keep my scholarship. The process to study and work abroad was complicated and I was constantly checking deadlines for visas. I knew that not everyone had the opportunities I did, so I wanted to make the most of it and not make any mistakes or take something for granted.

I studied hard and joined the Honors College. I also looked for leadership opportunities on campus and worked with a professor doing research in solar technology. I wanted to be as competitive as possible when applying for the engineering program.

When I was accepted, it was like my childhood dream was coming true. I continued studying hard and completed two internships in my senior year. When graduation came, I wanted to go home to see my parents, but knew I could keep expanding my career if I stayed. I applied for a work visa in the U.S. and was accepted to a large architectural engineering firm across the country. Now, I get to build skyscrapers and continue learning and growing in the career I love.

I think it is important that every college student try to volunteer or do an internship in their field of study. If I had not taken advantage of so many experiences such as research and working, I would not be doing what I am today. One of the corporations I interned with was how I connected with a large firm across the U.S. and got my job. I also think it is important that students enjoy what they are doing. Like I said, my family thought I was crazy when I was a little boy who said I would grow up to build things...and now they couldn't be prouder – and for that reason, I am proud too.

STUDENT SILHOUETTE: SIMI

I come from a single-parent household and have been working since high school. I begged my mom to let me leave high school and just get my GED. In the second semester of my junior year, she finally gave in. I dropped out in February and completed my GED in March. By the summer I applied to our local state college and worked throughout my college career, so I was not full-time every semester. I completed my Associate's degrees in 3 years and managed my time to keep good grades. I wasn't on campus often, but I explored different opportunities and clubs.

I transferred to a large, public university for my Bachelor degree. When I entered, I could tell from the start that it wasn't the right fit for me. I felt like I could not find the resources I needed and was overwhelmed by the large classes, large campus, and what felt like competition with other students. Along with that, I had personal challenges and was trying to navigate through the pandemic.

I decided that the best course of action would be to take a break from college and really figure out what I should do before trying again. I found myself longing for the experience I had at the state college that brought me so much confidence and connections. I researched what

Bachelor's degrees were offered (there were only a few since it is a state college) and knew that an education degree would be right for me so that I can help students like me who think of dropping out. I applied to the Bachelor's program at the state college and was accepted. Although I am not involved in the same ways I was while pursuing my Associate degree, I am happy to be back on the community college campus and have also accepted an internship and am working in a school to learn hands-on teaching skills.

I think sometimes the hardest part of college is finding the right fit for you personally – although it took a few tries, I am so happy I found the best college experience for me!

REFERENCES

Cordova, C. G. (2022). *The career decision-making self-efficacy and career action steps of humanities students: A quantitative survey analysis.* ProQuest Dissertations Publishing.

Costa, D. (2022). Bachelor degree. Encyclopedia Britannica. https://www.britannica.com/topic/bachelors-degree

Jaschik, S. (2023). Why students opt not to enroll. *Inside Higher Ed.* https://www.insidehighered.com/news/admissions/2023/06/12/why-students-opt-out-college?utm_source=Inside+Higher+Ed&utm_campaign=8f4624a2fb-DNU_2021_COPY_02&utm_medium=email&utm_term=0_1fcbc04421-8f4624a2fb-237827861&mc_cid=8f4624a2fb&mc_eid=5176a715a3

National Center for Education Statistics (NCES). (2023). Fast facts: Financial aid. Institute of Education Sciences. https://nces.ed.gov/fastfacts/display.asp?id=31

National Student Clearinghouse Research Center (NSCRC). (2023). Undergraduate degree earners. Academic year 2021–2022. National Student Clearinghouse. https://nscresearchcenter.org/undergraduate-degree-earners/

Schanzanbach, D. W., Turner, J. A., & Turner, S. (2023). Raising state minimum wages, lowering community college enrollment. National Bureau of Economic Research. http://www.nber.org/papers/w31540

The United States Census Bureau. (2022). A higher degree. U.S. Census Bureau, U.S. Department of Commerce. https://www.census.gov/library/visualizations/2022/comm/a-higher-degree.html

IN CONSIDERATION OF MASTER'S OR DOCTORAL DEGREES

ABSTRACT

Chapter 7 outlines some pros and cons of seeking an advanced degree. It includes descriptions of teaching assistants, supplemental instructors, and various other terms associated with graduate education. In addition, it gives a glimpse of the current employment trends for advanced degrees. The Student Silhouette in this chapter is a student who completed her veterinary degree.

WHAT EVEN ARE MASTER'S AND DOCTORAL DEGREES?

Master's and **Doctoral** degrees are considered advanced degrees that require an additional two to four years of school after completing your undergraduate baccalaureate degree; 24.1% of Americans hold a Master's degree, and less than 5% of the U.S. holds a Doctoral degree (U.S. Census Bureau, 2022). One thing to note about **graduate degrees** is that they cost much more per credit (sometimes double!) than undergraduate degrees. This means that after you spend four years of your life and thousands of dollars on your undergraduate degree, you are now rewarded with higher course fees, more studying, and more time in college! Obviously, this is not the right choice for everyone.

DOI: 10.4324/9781032692258-7

WHY WOULD YOU GET A MASTER OR DOCTORAL DEGREE?

If you really enjoy studying and want to complete research in your field, a **terminal degree** (the highest degree in your field) may be the right choice for you. Graduate degrees offer specialization and expertise in different areas of study. Additionally, earning a graduate degree allows you more time to study things you are passionate about and potentially research and publish articles about them. Faculty help you narrow your focus so that you can explore new topics and expand related literature and research. Graduate classes are smaller and often offered at times that would allow you to study and work. However, certain programs (especially those in the field of medicine) require residencies, where you get hands-on experience working in the field. **Residencies** often require long hours associated with lower wages while students are immersed in the workplace environment.

Earning a higher degree does not come without additional costs. Although a graduate degree often equates to higher wages, this is not always the case. Without prior work experience, even someone with a Master degree can start at an entry-level position at entry-level wages. This is why getting related work experience before starting in a career is so important! It is also vital to research the field you plan on pursuing so that you can determine whether or not an additional degree is actually necessary. Certain careers may not require or reward higher education. For example, 73% of radiologic technologists and technicians have Associate's degrees, and 17% work in the field with a certificate (Career Coach, 2023). On the other hand, 81% of dentists hold a Doctoral degree or more and earn an annual average salary of about $125,000 (Career Coach, 2023).

GRADUATE DEGREE OPPORTUNITIES

Although graduate degrees are costly in time and resources, you can help offset the increased fees by asking about **graduate assistantship** opportunities within your field. "Grad" assistantships are when the college pays for your coursework *and* pays you a salary! This sounds like a great way to get a free Master degree! But not so fast … in return for free classes and a salary, you generally work teaching lower-level introductory courses as a **teaching assistant (TA)** or **supplemental instructor (SI)**. In this role, your classes are paid for and you are employed on campus helping to teach. Thus, assistantships are a good option if you plan on continuing to teach at the collegiate level, but they may not be the best fit if you are seeking higher wages or may not want to teach. Still, if you have any aspirations of continuing your education to the Doctoral level (**Ph.D.**, **Ed.D.**), you will want to ensure you seek out assistantship opportunities and consider what scholarships and funding may be available.

When you are accepted and enrolled in a graduate degree program, you will meet with a Faculty Advisor who will present a framework or pathway for your degree completion. Although broader in opportunities, graduate degrees often follow structured curricula that allow you to narrow your learning and delve deeply into a field of interest. Before pursuing a graduate degree, you will want to make sure that you are committed and interested in studying your chosen area for at least two years of research, labs, and writing.

Also, be sure to explore work opportunities in the field prior to applying. Some Doctoral degrees (such as a Doctor of Medicine, M.D.) are streamlined with certain classes that must be taken in a certain way and completed with a paid residency or work experience in a hospital. However, not all Doctoral degrees are as structured with specific class pathways and you should not assume more schooling leads to more money. For example, with a 59% unemployment rate (Hartman, 2020), Ph.D. graduates in the humanities may do better to go directly into the workforce rather than continue their education. In fact, the job prospects for humanities Ph.D. students are so dismal that some educators are calling for a two-year hiatus in Doctoral admissions (Hartman, 2020).

An important thing to note regarding advanced degrees is that anyone with a "Ph.D." or "M.D." or "D.O." behind their name is referred to as **Dr.** However, these "doctors" are quite different. A person with a Ph.D. is a Doctor of Philosophy. This means that they can have a terminal degree in any field … not just philosophy. They are considered a "philosophical doctor." So if someone has a Ph.D. in biology or history, they are called "doctor" because of their "Doctor of Philosophy" degree. Likewise, individuals with a Ph.D. are the ones doing research in a certain field. A "M.D." doctor, on the other hand, is a medical doctor who helps improve the health or medical condition of individuals. Think of it this way: a Doctor of Philosophy is doing the research that helps the Doctor of Medicine to treat patients and write prescriptions.

Although a more advanced degree sets you apart in a field, it still comes with cost and risk. Plus, pursuing higher education indicates more time, money, energy, and alas … homework. With more students seeking higher degrees, the market becomes saturated and thus devalues the advanced degree. If employers do not value the degree, then the risk of paying for more education may not be worth it. Be sure to do your research and confirm that more schooling is the right path for you before pursuing any higher level of education.

STUDENT SILHOUETTE: SHANELLE

My undergraduate experience was a little more party than study. It wasn't until my senior year that I really found out what I wanted to do – I wanted to become a veterinarian and work with large animals. Unfortunately, all of my partying meant my grades were not good enough to apply. Therefore, I worked hard to retake certain courses and had to prolong my undergraduate experience taking new ones that prepared me for vet school.

After an extra full year, I applied and was accepted. I knew that this time I was going to study hard. I went to a public university for my Bachelor's degree and a public university for my D.V.M. (Doctor of Veterinary Medicine). Just like other Doctoral programs, I had to take lots of classes and complete a residency where I worked in the field. Unfortunately, my residency barely paid enough for me to live on with food, rent, and classes … but I at least I loved working with the horses and cattle.

When I graduated, my residency preparation and training made it easy for me to find a well-paying job. I have been able to pay off my undergraduate class debt but still have veterinary school bills that I pay monthly.

I wish I had buckled down sooner and thought about what I wanted to study instead of partying so much in my first three years. I feel like I had two extreme experiences: one with all partying and one with all studying. My friends told me that there was a happy median, but I should have listened to them sooner. Still, working as a veterinarian is the best job I could have ever imagined. Although it took extra time, classes, and money, it was worth it for me to find the career I love.

REFERENCES

Career Coach. (2023). Career coach. Emsi. www.fsw.emsicc.com

Hartman, S. (2020). A pause in the pandemic. *Inside Higher Ed.* https://www.insidehighered.com/advice/2020/08/18/grad-schools-should-halt-doctoraladmissions-humanities-two-years-opinion

The United States Census Bureau. (2022). A higher degree. U.S. Census Bureau, U.S. Department of Commerce. https://www.census.gov/library/visualizations/2022/comm/a-higher-degree.html

MICROCREDENTIALING AND INDUSTRY CERTIFICATIONS FOR EXTRA SKILLS

ABSTRACT

Chapter 8 outlines many of the current industry trends and certifications such as microcredentials and badges. These college alternative options are industry-recognized credentials that can lead to employment gains through skill learning and development. This chapter offers the economic outlook and perceptions related to these terms and provides a Student Silhouette of someone who found certifications as a valuable alternative to traditional college and career experiences.

MICRO ... WHAT?

Since the 1970s students have believed that pursuing higher education would in fact help them get a better job (The Chronicle of Higher Education, 2022). Although 87% of employers believe a college degree is valuable, only six in ten employers felt as though recent graduates possessed the necessary skills for entry-level positions in their organizations (AAC&U, 2021). Sixty-five percent of current employers feel recent graduates are lacking soft skills and 46% believe they do not have the necessary technology skills (Shireman, 2023). This means that students are pursuing and graduating from college with the expectation of career readiness; however, they are coming up short. Whether this is due to personal deficiency or university lack of preparation, the evidence remains that college graduates are not meeting employers' expectations.

DOI: 10.4324/9781032692258-8

For this reason, many employers are seeking non-traditional qualifications associated with their industry. Increasingly, industry certifications such as **microcredentials** have become more popular among employers and employees. Microcredentials, or targeted skills-based trainings (literally meaning small credits), present an alternative qualification for employees within an industry. Successful completion of a microcredential is represented with a digital **badge** to serve as the online emblem for completion. Microcredential courses are often offered online and meant to provide "small" (micro) skills-based trainings in the format of a short course, lecture, or project that exposes you to an aspect of an industry or a workforce skill. For example, you may complete a series of workshops on Microsoft Office Suite in order to earn a credential. You could also complete a communication course and receive a badge verifying your exposure to interpersonal skills.

Industry certifications, such as microcredentials can be earned prior to employment or concurrently. What's more, some employers may pay for employees to pursue industry certifications in tandem with employment or higher education as a means of diversifying skillsets and stacking credentials (Fong et al., 2023). Microcredentials are short trainings (think skill certifications) that can enhance your degree and can be added to your résumé for marketability. Certain industries prefer students to have skills related to their exact fields; microcredentials are a great way to demonstrate gained career skills outside of regular coursework and classes. You can add them to your online LinkedIn profile and list them on your résumé as an earned badge. Although microcredentials are a popular trend in employment training, they should not be considered certification within a field. Microcredentials can be offered within or outside a given industry. Employers, schools, and universities all offer skills-based trainings that can be applied to various workplaces. Remember that microcredentials are designed for skill-based training to help you develop career skills.

LET'S LOOK AT THE DATA WITH THIS EMERGING TREND

On average, 88% of employers believe a microcredential strengthens a candidate's application and are 72% more likely to hire a candidate who has a microcredential (Shireman, 2023). Furthermore, 74% of employers feel that an industry microcredential improves performance in entry-level positions (Shireman, 2023). This is perhaps why 48% of Human Resources (HR) executives report witnessing or hiring job candidates with industry-related badges (1EdTech, 2021). Thus, many employers value microcredentials as evidence of attention to workplace skills.

Another important industry certification is a **professional certificate**. Professional certificates are certificates that can be issued online or on paper as a means of "certifying" your earned knowledge and credentials. Certificates are gained through longer courses that provide background information in an industry alongside skill development. These credentials may involve topic exams or an overall exam to verify learning and understanding. Unlike microcredentials which may be created outside an industry, professional certificates are often created and certified within an industry, so they are considered to be verified qualifications for a specific field. Some certificates can be combined with microcredential badges to demonstrate knowledge and skills in an industry and specific area. They are also stackable and in demand. According to the National Student Clearinghouse Resource Center, first-time certificate earners was the only area of undergraduate degree increase, with 9% expansion (2023). This means that either in place of or in addition to pursuing a degree, students are ensuring that they are certified in given areas in order to enhance their employability within an industry.

Data supports that both students and future employees also seem to find value in microcredentials and professional certificates. Ninety percent of students and recent graduates believe that industry certifications such as a microcredential make them more competitive applicants and would be more likely to enroll in a program that offered an industry credential (Shireman, 2023). Likewise, in a survey sponsored by the University Professional and Continuing Education Association (UPCEA) and Collegis Education, 81% of HR professionals cited incentivizing employees to gain additional industry certifications, with 68% providing tuition reimbursement, 39% offering education release time, and 65% confirming the increased likelihood of promotional opportunities (Fong et al., 2023). For these reasons, more students are stacking their credentials and foregoing college for certifications in the workplace.

CREDENTIALS ... NOT DEGREES

Although microcredentials and other industry certifications are effective ways to gain industry knowledge, skills-based trainings and professional certifications do not guarantee employment and are still not regarded as replacements for degrees. Given the fact that microcredentials can be created in many industries outside their application, recent research is demonstrating employer skepticism related to the quality and standardization of badging (Fong et al., 2023). Whereas degrees come with accrediting support and rigorous metrics, microcredentials that are not always industry-specific and can be offered in areas such as "emotional intelligence" and "teamwork." Many employers consider these skills to be inherently earned or workplace-developed and can doubt badge quality and validity – even if the skills they advertise are in demand. Therefore, it is important to consider the value of an industry certification prior to exploration. Additionally, you can research employer-specific certifications to confirm you are seeking qualifications they value within their own company. In fact, many large technology companies and organizations host their own credentialing programs to ensure quality and standardization.

Given the debate over industry-specific quality, it is important to consider the overall value of career skill development. Whether the certifications were earned while in college or in the workforce, more than half of employers believe that résumés containing alternative credentials such as microcredentialing or certifications show evidence of willingness for skill development, initiative, communicated competencies, and up-to-date knowledge (Fong et al., 2023). This means that even if you earn a badge or certification in an area outside of your work industry, the demonstration of interest, motivation, and gained skills are still appealing to employers. Therefore, if you decide to pursue an industry certification such as a microcredential or a professional certificate, research its value and application in various industries and fields of work. Gaining industry certifications requires your time, effort, and resources and you want to make sure the outcome is valued and recognized by your employer.

STUDENT SILHOUETTE: KAYLYNN

I watched my mom struggle to pay off her student loan debt for years for a degree that she didn't use in her daily life. I knew that I never wanted to have that feeling. So when I graduated from high school, I decided to go into the workforce rather than college.

One of my mom's friends told me that her business was hiring and that I should apply to be a pharmacy technician. I didn't know what this was at first; but after some research, I found out that I could earn a certificate and begin my career. Completing the certificate program was relatively simple – I took courses online and passed the necessary exam. I actually started working in the job my mom's friend told me about before I completed my certification and they paid for me to take the classes and exam. I've been in the role for two years now and can't imagine doing anything else. I assist the pharmacist and patients with their prescriptions and learn about dosage, chemicals, and medication names.

What I like most about my job is feeling like I am helping people get better. Rather than sitting in a classroom taking notes on things I am not interested in, I am counting dosage, confirming prescriptions, and working a stable job with promotional opportunities.

Working this job has given me a new-found appreciation for pharmacy and healthcare. After talking with the pharmacist, I am thinking of pursuing some medication certifications and pharmacy classes to explore the industry and learn more about the field. One day I may become a pharmacist – but right now I am happy as a pharmacy technician helping people feel better and getting them the help they need.

REFERENCES

American Association of Colleges and Universities (AAC&U). (2021). How college contributes to workforce success. AAC&U, 1–39. https://www.aacu.org/sites/default/files/files/research/AACUEmployerReport2021.pdf

Fong, J., Etter, B., & Sullberg, D. (2023). The effect of employer understanding and engagement on non-degree credentials. University Professional and Continuing Education Association (UPCEA) and Collegis Education, Inc. https://upcea.edu/wp-content/uploads/2023/05/The-Effect-of-Employer-Understanding-and-Engagement-on-Non-Degree-Credentials_UPCEA-and-Collegis_February-2023.pdf

National Student Clearinghouse Research Center (NSCRC). (2023). Undergraduate degree earners. Academic year 2021–2022. National Student Clearinghouse. https://nscresearchcenter.org/undergraduate-degree-earners/

Shireman, S. (2023). New Coursera survey shows high demand for industry micro-credentials from students and employers in tight labor market. Coursera for Campus. https://blog.coursera.org/from-higher-education-to-employment/

The Chronicle of Higher Education. (2022). Building tomorrow's work force. What employers want you to know. The Chronicle of Higher Education, Inc.

1EdTech Foundation. (2021). Digital credentials and competency frameworks: Exploring employer readiness and use in talent management. 1EdTech Foundation and IMS Global Learning Consortium, Inc. https://www.imsglobal.org/sites/default/files/wellspring/Wellspring_II_Employer_Research.pdf

ACADEMIC AND INDUSTRY TERMS TO CLEAR THE CONFUSION

ABSTRACT

This chapter contains over 100 common academic and industry terms.

Rather than spend too much time explaining *why* students and parents need to understand these terms, it seems more tangible and most pragmatic to list them with the intention of allowing you to seek out the ones you may not know. Whether you attend a four-year or two-year college or university, higher education institutions often make the unfortunate assumption that every incoming student and their parent(s) are inherently aware of academic terms and processes. Likewise, there are many new career and workplace terms that have become popularized given industry changes. For this reason, the glossary below, though not exhaustive, is meant to be a helpful tool for understanding common jargon and acronyms related to your college choice.

COMMON TERMS OFTEN ASSOCIATED WITH HIGHER EDUCATION AND CAREER DECISION-MAKING

- Academic Advisor – Individual(s) responsible for helping students select courses to work toward graduation by assisting in course enrollment and discussing degree options and requirements.
- Academic Affairs – The division within an institution responsible for academic-related decisions including curriculum. This area is overseen by the Provost.

DOI: 10.4324/9781032692258-9

- Accelerated Program – An academic area of study that is offered in an expedited amount of time with shorter classes and more flexibility.
- Accreditation – The process by which an institution is considered qualified to be offering higher education instruction. The accreditation transfers to qualifications of student degrees and diplomas so it is *very* important that students ensure an institution is accredited.
- Adaptive Services – Resource center for students with accessibility needs or documented disabilities. In college/university, students must self-identify with this office.
- Add/Drop Period – The amount of time in the semester (generally a week) that allows students to change their class schedule without payment or GPA penalty.
- Adjunct – Part-time or temporarily employed instructor or professor.
- Admissions – The office responsible for reviewing applications and accepting students to the institution.
- Apprenticeship – A paid opportunity to work and learn in a given field or industry that often involves direct, hands-on learning and relevant training.
- Associate of Applied Science (AAS) – A unique degree that prepares students for a specific job by teaching industry skills within specific fields. This degree often has active coursework and industry exposure. This is often for entry-level positions.
- Associate of Arts (AA) – A degree (generally two years) that includes general education courses and may easily transfer to a college or university for credit.
- Associate of Occupational Studies (AOS) – A unique degree that prepares students for a specific job by teaching industry skills within specific fields. This is often for entry-level positions.
- Associate of Science (AS) – A degree (generally two years) that is more vocationally focused. A student may have additional general education requirements to complete if transferring to a college/university.
- Associate degree – A two-year degree to prepare for a Bachelor degree.
- Asynchronous – Fully online course.

- Attrition – Data related to the number of students who do not return to the institution over a period of time.
- Bachelor of Arts degree (BA) – A four-year Bachelor degree focused outside of a STEM field.
- Baccalaureate degree – four-year degree (synonymous with Bachelor's degrees).
- Badging – An online emblem or documentation to verify completion of a skills-based credential such as a microcredential training or certificate program.
- Bachelor of Science (BS) – A four-year Bachelor degree focused in a STEM field.
- Bachelor of Science/Art (BSA) – A four-year Bachelor degree focused in STEM and Art fields.
- Bachelor of Science in Nursing (BSN) – A Bachelor degree focused in nursing.
- Bursar – Office responsible for student fees and charges.
- Cabinet – The highest level of leadership at an institution. This often includes Presidents and Vice Presidents.
- Career and Technical Education (CTE) – Courses and education designed to offer skills and credentials so that students can begin their careers and go directly into the workforce. This term is often used interchangeably with vocational education.
- Cashier – Office responsible for collecting and charging student fees.
- Certificate – An earned documentation related to skills-based training completion.
- Chair – Lead faculty of a department.
- Co-curricular/Co-curricular Transcript – Out-of-class activities are sometimes listed on a separate transcript.
- College – This term can also be applied to an area of study and combined courses at a university (i.e., College of Education, College of Engineering, etc.).
- Commencement – Graduation ceremony.
- Common Application – College/University application that requires general information and can be sent to multiple institutions.
- Community/State College – A college that offers primarily two-year degrees.

- Concentration – An area of focus within a major.
- Continuing Education – This term often refers to students who are returning to education after taking a break.
- Continuing Generation – This term often refers to students whose parents graduated from a higher education institution.
- Convocation – Ceremony that welcomes faculty/staff/students to campus at the beginning of the semester or year.
- Co-requisite – A course required to be taken at the same time as another course.
- Course Reference Number (CRN) – The unique number assigned to each course section.
- Credit/Credit Hour – The number of applied hours for a course. Degree programs have hour requirements that students must meet in order to graduate. Each course has an hour applied. Most courses are three credit hours in college.
- Curriculum – Required coursework related to completing a degree.
- Dean – Higher-ranking faculty member, above the Chair of a department, who is responsible for an entire college department or area of study.
- Deferred Admission – The option for a student to delay beginning higher education (synonymous with deferred enrollment).
- Deferred Enrollment – The option for a student to delay beginning higher education (synonymous with deferred admission).
- Degree – Completed requirements within an area or field of student for graduation.
- Diploma – The paper signifying an earned degree. Diplomas are not often given at graduation; rather students receive a diploma cover and are mailed a diploma once all fees have been paid and the Office of the Registrar confirms all graduation requirements have been met.
- Discipline – Field of study.
- Dissertation – Coursework and final paper associated with doctoral-level education that includes much research, study, and preparation.
- Doctorate – Highest academic degree in a given field.
- Doctor of Philosophy (Ph.D.) – A terminal degree applied to any field (Philosophy and otherwise) and bears the title, Dr.

- Dr. – Term applied to any individual holding the highest degree in their field. This could include Ph.D., Ed.D., M.D., D.O., D.V.M., etc.
- Dual Enrollment – The opportunity for students to take college-level courses for college-level credit while still in high school.
- Doctor of Osteopathic Medicine (D.O.) – A terminal degree for a doctor of osteopathic medicine.
- Doctor of Veterinary Medicine (D.V.M.) – A terminal degree qualifying a veterinarian.
- Early Action – An expedited, non-binding decision related to college admissions.
- Early Decision – An expedited, binding decision related to college admissions.
- Education Doctorate (Ed.D.) – Credentials signifying Doctorate in Education.
- Elective – Course options to take within a certain area of study that will count toward graduation requirements.
- Experiential – Learning that is considered to include "experiences" and action-oriented learning.
- Externship – An unpaid job shadowing opportunity with an organization or within an industry.
- Faculty – Qualified/Credentialed group of individuals within a college/university division or area of study who are expected to teach and do research within their field.
- Federal Education Privacy Act form (FERPA) – An act protecting your private education information so that colleges/universities cannot give out your information without your consent.
- Free Application for Federal Student Aid (FAFSA) – This form can be found *only* on the government website and should be completed *each* year in order for a student to qualify for any federal financial aid the next year.
- Financial Aid – Funding assistance applied for a student to complete higher education. It can be federal or institution-specific, including scholarships and loans.
- First-Generation – Any student whose parents did not complete a four-year Bachelor degree. This term applies even if siblings completed a Bachelor degree.
- First-Time-in-College (FTIC) – A term given to any student who is starting their college or university career at the

institution. This term is still applied to students who completed Advanced Placement (AP) or Dual Enrollment (DE) credits. Generally, if the student is enrolled in their first full year at the institution (and no longer enrolled in high school) they are considered FTIC.

- For-Profit College – An institution that is designed using a business model and operated by a company with stakeholders seeking revenue in return for students' investment. These schools do not usually receive federal funding or aid.
- Foundation – The office responsible for fundraising for a college/university.
- Full-time – An enrollment term for students who pursue at least 12 credits in a semester.
- Graduate Equivalency Degree or General Education Diploma (GED) – Certificate assigned to students who complete a test that qualifies them as obtaining high school-level equivalent education.
- General Education/Core Education – A variety or sequence of courses required for graduation based on necessary curriculum.
- Grade Point Average (GPA) – The average of a student's grades, MOST affected a student's first year of college.
- Graduate Assistantship (GA) – A funding opportunity for graduate-level students to work at the institution and be reimbursed for their graduate coursework.
- Graduate Degree – A degree post-Bachelor degree that requires more schooling, such as a Master degree.
- Graduate Record Examination (GRE) – A required test for various graduate/Master's degrees programs admissions.
- Hispanic Service Institution (HIS) – A college or university with 25% or more undergraduate full-time enrollment of Hispanic or Latin students.
- Historically Black College and/or University (HBCU) – A college or university established before the Civil Rights Act of 1964, to serve primarily African American students.
- Humanities – Areas of study related to human experiences such as English, Philosophy, Anthropology, History, etc.
- Incomplete – A grade that can be applied after an appeal process given extenuating circumstances that allows a student to complete a course after the semester/term ends.

- Instructor – A college professor without tenure.
- Internship – A paid or unpaid opportunity to work and learn in a given field or industry.
- Juris Doctor (JD) – A terminal degree for law.
- Land Grant Institution – A college or university established through federal funding from the Morrill Act (1862) which offers agricultural and mechanic courses.
- Lecturer – A guest speaker or instructor without tenure.
- Liberal Arts – Areas of study related to the Humanities rooted in classical education.
- Liberal Arts College – Usually a private college that is designed to offer a broad and holistic education requiring certain courses for degree and graduation requirements.
- Master in Arts (MA) – A graduate degree focused outside a STEM field.
- Major – Area of focus or study within a field.
- Master in Science (MS) – A graduate degree focused in a STEM field.
- Master in Business Administration (MBA) – A graduate degree in the field of Business.
- Master in Fine Arts (MFA) – A terminal degree, considered the highest in the field of arts.
- Master in Social Work (MSW) – A graduate degree, qualifying a social worker.
- Medical Doctor (M.D.) – A terminal degree in the field of medicine.
- Microcredential – A program or training designed to offer industry-specific skills gained outside of general college coursework.
- Minor – An area of study or specialization within a major that includes required courses and a certain number of credits within that field.
- Non-traditional learner – A student who is taking classes after a period of break or who has not pursued higher education before and is not considered traditional college-age.
- Office hours – Time that professors are required to spend in their office in order to meet with students. Take advantage of this time to stop in and visit them!
- Orientation – An introduction to the institution through an online or in-person requirement.

- Part-time – An enrollment term for students who pursue fewer than 12 credits in a semester.
- Pell Grant – A Federal grant awarded to undergraduate students in need of financial aid. This financial grant is need-based determined by FAFSA completion and does not need to be repaid.
- Plagiarism – Academic cheating.
- Post-secondary – A term synonymous with higher education to mean after high school.
- Pre-requisite – A course required to be taken prior to another course. Certain courses are sequenced.
- President – The highest level of leadership at an institution.
- Private College – An institution that is designed for education and is funded through private sources. It may receive federal tax breaks and offer federal aid.
- Professor – Expert teaching in the field of study, often with tenure.
- Provost – The Chief Academic Officer, responsible for overseeing faculty, Academic Affairs, and subjects related to academic programs and policies.
- Public University – A higher education institution designed for education and controlled through federal and state funding.
- Registrar – Office responsible for registration options such as course offerings. This office also processes transcripts to determine course credit hours, graduation requirements, etc.
- Residence Life – The housing on campus, often referred to as dorms and associated facilities.
- Residency Status – A term applied to whether or not a student is considered to be a resident of the state. Residency Status must be applied for and is not guaranteed, even if a student graduated within the state.
- Residencies – Postgraduate training programs within a workplace environment.
- Retention – Data related to the number of students who remain at the institution over a period of time (antonym of attrition).
- Scholarship – A term applied to research or a term applied to any financial aid that does not require repayment.
- Semester/Semester Hour – The time related to academic study, often 15–18 weeks.

- Skilled job – a job that requires specific knowledge and aptitude related to the necessary tasks of the job.
- Stafford Loan – Federal fixed-rate financial aid subsidized loan opportunity for students pursuing higher education.
- Student Affairs – The division within an institution responsible for student-related decisions including residence life, clubs, organizations, resources, etc.
- Subsidized Loan – Financial aid loan opportunity that does not accrue interest while a student is actively pursuing higher education at the undergraduate level.
- Supplemental Instructor (SI) – Another term for a TA, though a SI may be an undergraduate student.
- Teaching Assistant (TA) – An individual (often a graduate student) who assists a professor in teaching a course.
- Tenure – Credential earned by faculty to remain in a position with teaching status.
- Term – The course of time related to academic study, often used synonymously with semester. However, terms may be a quarter of a semester.
- Terminal degree – The highest degree achievable within a given field or area of study.
- Thesis – Coursework and final paper associated with graduate-level education that includes much research, study, and preparation.
- Test of English as a Foreign Language (TOEFL) – A test for non-native English speakers to assist in determining course placement.
- Trade job – A job that often requires specific skills and aptitudes related to tasks performed on the job and knowledge within the industry.
- Transfer – A term used to describe a student who completed coursework at a different college/university and is continuing education at a new college or university. Some colleges only consider a student who completed 60 credit hours or more to be a transfer rather than first-time-in-college (FTIC).
- Transcript – A list of completed, required courses at an institution.
- Transient – A term used to describe a student who is enrolled in one institution but completing a course or two at another

institution for college credit. This term does not apply to Dual Enrollment (DE) students who are still enrolled in high school.

- Tuition – The combination of required course fees and student fees for a semester/term (i.e., the cost of attending college).
- Undergraduate degree – An Associate or Bachelor degree.
- Unsubsidized Loan – Financial aid loan opportunity that accrues interest and can be used for undergraduate or graduate education.
- Vocational Education – Courses and education designed to offer skills and credentials so that students can begin their careers and go directly into the workforce. This term is often used interchangeably with CTE.
- Waitlist – A term applied to students waiting to be accepted to an institution or course.
- Withdraw Period – The amount of time in the semester (generally about halfway) that allows students to change or remove a class from their schedule. Withdrawing from a course does require course payment but does show up on a student's transcript. The course grade is listed as a "W" and does not impact a student's GPA. Certain financial scholarships only allow a limited number of withdrawals so it is important to consult Academic Advising and Financial Aid prior to withdrawing from a course.

For an additional resource, see Slyter, K. (2019). The Ultimate glossary of college terminology. Rasmussen University.

REFERENCE

Slyter, K. (2019). The ultimate glossary of college terminology. Rasmussen University. https://www.rasmussen.edu/student-experience/college-life/college-terminology-glossary/

10

CONCLUSION
Choosing What's Right for You

ABSTRACT

This final chapter encompasses a brief synopsis and overview of the text. It provides general reminders and the important takeaway that: "the process of deciding whether or not to attend college may be life-changing, but it can also change throughout life. Deciding on a college does not directly determine your future. Deciding on a major does not determine your future. What determines the future is YOU!"

WHAT DOES THIS MEAN FOR THE FUTURE WORKFORCE?

Higher education and the opportunities it provides are a dynamic and ever-changing landscape impacted by shifting economic and workforce trends. Changes in wages, labor markets, inflation, and employment rates all contribute to shaping opportunities, costs, and risks associated with college decision-making (De Brey et al., 2021; Schanzenbach et al., 2023). Since the pandemic, enrollment has declined across all levels of higher education (Jaschik, 2023), but perhaps most shocking is *how* it has declined: Undergraduate male college attendance declined more than females in every racial and ethnic group since 2020 (The Chronicle of Higher Education, 2021). Whether economically, socially, or personally motivated, fewer men are pursuing degrees than in the past, which will add to disparities in the workforce. This means that while fewer men are attending college, workplaces that require degrees are becoming

DOI: 10.4324/9781032692258-10

less diverse. This diversity issue could be extended further as 82% of business leaders expect humans and machines to be working collaboratively as a team in their company within five years (Dell Technologies & IFTF, 2023).

Historically and across cultures, financial achievement, job security, promotional opportunities, a pleasant working environment, social networks, recognition, and work/life balance have all been associated with career success (Demel et al., 2012) In fact, as supported by the research of Katz and Kahn (1978), careers are linked to identity development and fulfillment (Briscoe et al., 2012). Perhaps you have heard the famous saying attributed to philosopher Confucius: Choose a job you love and you will never work a day in your life. Although the premise is positive (and most nurses, teachers, and social workers may agree that they love helping others), the quote seems to imply that if you do not love what you do, you will dislike work every day of your life. Your decision regarding your career does not have to be so extreme. While arguments for the need for appropriate career education remain relevant in contemporary society, higher education may no longer be the expected pathway to starting a career. Thirty-four percent of human resource leaders (23% more than three years ago) admitted to skills-based hiring strategies that value competencies rather than solely degrees (1EdTech, 2021). It seems to follow as reasoning for why only 20% of employers cited college/university transcripts as useful, 24% very useful, and 20% extremely useful (1EdTech, 2021).

What's perhaps more daunting is more recent data collected by the HEA Group, a college education research consultancy working in policy development, data analysis, and government relations (HEA, 2024). The agency conducted research using U.S. Department of Education College Scorecard data to analyze the median wage earnings of 5 million students across 3,887 institutions, ten years after their initial college enrollment. According to the report, 8% of the institutions had students earning less than $21,870 of annual income, 22% had former students earning below $15 minimum wage, and 26% had former students who were earning less than a typical high school graduate of $32,000 per year (HEA, 2024).

YIKES

But if you are choosing to go to college, do not let this dissuade you. It is important to remember that depending on your source, there are about 6,000 different colleges and universities to choose from in the U.S. alone – not counting higher education alternatives; this data is only representative of a select number of institutions. Additionally, the report does not include demographic information or confirmation if the students actually graduated and in what fields. Information like this is important to highlight *why* these might be the wage earnings noted of the former student populations.

What is evident, however, is that in order for higher education to remain relevant in the twenty-first century and beyond, it must continue to navigate pedagogical and economic spaces with an insistence upon relevancy, adoption, and adaptability without losing its roots in holistic instruction. As author Robert Newman (2021) argues, "Only with a turn toward the pragmatic might the esoteric be safely preserved and nurtured" (para. 5). This is a challenging task not simply solved through workplace badging. Rather, it is crucial that higher education remain pragmatic for all students while remaining committed to curiosity and exploration.

SELECTING *YOUR* PATH

As I noted in the Preface, going through the college/university decision process is often a stressful time filled with an overwhelming sense of choices. There is a lot of work, effort, and anxiety that goes into decision-making, applications, and tasks. Despite the title of this text, you should not think that choosing whether or not to attend college is a binary decision – there are lots of options when making the choice. Perhaps you get some college credits, join the workforce, and then go back to higher education. Perhaps you join the workforce and then start college as a non-traditional student after establishing a career and family. And perhaps you never go to college but become an entrepreneur with your own company that drives your happiness and success. No matter your choice, know that you can keep choosing different paths and options to create the future you hope to achieve. Remember along the way that family, friends, teachers, mentors, co-workers, and leaders, can all help inspire you in your decisions – but ultimately you decide what is best for your goals.

Higher education creates opportunities. It allows you personal, academic, and professional growth and exploration. College students have the latitude to engage in diversity, research, partying, scholarship, comradery, intellectual inquiry, collaboration, resource acquisition, and learning in an inimitable and exciting way. Critical thinking and academic investigation behave uniquely on college campuses and provide enhanced rhetoric and diverse dialogue that are exclusive to university life. Students live, study, and work together alongside other scholars engaged in academic inquiry. It provides a motivating setting that without a doubt leads to intellectual growth.

When considering whether or not to pursue higher education, you should recognize that college is most enjoyed when most utilized. At no other time in your adult life will you have the same access to resources, support, and scholarship. It would seem a waste for someone to be miserable when surrounded by so much opportunity; yet, it is equally as wasteful for a student to attend simply for a qualification that may not be necessary for their future professional goals. Thus, as in most things, the decision is very personal. It can be right for some and wrong for others. But what is wrong for all is to not do due diligence in necessary research and preparation so that the best decision can be made. Remember, college is not for everyone – but it was never intended to be, either.

Still, students' professional growth on college campuses is much more varied. If you are confident in your career and confident that it requires a two or four-year degree, then higher education should be your pursuit. But if you have strong reservations regarding a college or university, or if you are looking for an easier transition to higher education after high school, a community/state college is a better option. Two-year schools provide academic degrees that will transfer to colleges and universities seamlessly. In addition, they offer degrees that provide vocational credentials that transfer directly to the workforce. Community/state colleges also provide many of the same resources and same courses as colleges and universities – but at a smaller cost. Thus, if you are unsure whether or not a four-year commitment is the right commitment, two years to explore and decide upon future options is a great alternative. State and community colleges, along with trade schools, fill a vital need in helping students transition from high school to college and help to fill gaps in the workforce.

Nevertheless, if you truly have no inherent interest in pursuing higher education, then it is in your best interest to begin vocational exploration through training, volunteerism, and certifications. Colleges and universities were not initially intended to be the workforce gateway for every student, and they cannot fulfill this role adequately for everyone. Therefore, you must personally assess whether or not higher education aligns with your future goals. If you believe it would be a waste of time and resources to attend college, and if your engagement at a university would reflect this belief, then you are far better suited to go directly into the workforce and begin to build your career. Be proud of your choice! You may not be doing what your friends are doing in college, but you are making the brave choice to pursue your own goals. You have decided to contribute to the workforce now and will continue assessing your contribution as you move through your future career choices and promotions. As has been stated before, college is not for everyone and was not designed to be. So consider your options and make an educated decision based on your future career plans.

GO FOR IT!

If there is one important takeaway to this text, it is that the process of deciding whether or not to attend college may be life-changing, but it can also change throughout life. Deciding on a college does not directly determine your future. Deciding on a major does not determine your future. What determines the future is *You*! Therefore, you must equip yourself with as much research and knowledge as you need to feel confident moving forward with whatever decision you make. Remember, exposure is an answer to anxiety (Johnson & Ridley, 2004), so taking the risk of enrolling in college, or starting a certificate program, or beginning an apprenticeship in a related career field, will help you make progress toward your final goal. Begin researching and learning about your future now and continue learning as you go.

Good luck my friend!

REFERENCES

Briscoe, J. P., Hall, D. T., & Mayrhofer, W. (2012). *Careers around the world*. Routledge.

De Brey, C., Snyder, T. D., Zhang, A., & Dillow, S. A. (2021). Digest of education statistics 2019. National Center for Education Statistics, American Institutes for Research, and U.S. Department of Education. https://nces.ed.gov/pubs2021/2021009.pdf

Dell Technologies & Institute for the Future (IFTF). (2023). Realizing 2030: A divided vision of the future. Dell Technologies. https://www.delltechnologies.com/content/dam/delltechnologies/assets/perspectives/2030/pdf/Realizing-2030-A-Divided-Vision-of-the-Future-Summary.pdf

Demel, B., Shen, Y., Las Heras, M., Hall, D. T., & Unite, J. (2012). Career success around the world: Its meaning and perceived influences in 11 countries. In J. P. Briscoe, D. T. Hall, & W. Mayrhofer (Eds.), *Careers around the world* (pp. 59–87). Routledge.

HEA Group. (2024). Ensuring a living wage through higher education. The HEA Group. www.theheagroup.com/blog/ensuring-a-living-wage-through-higher-education

Jaschik, S. (2023). Why students opt not to enroll. *Inside Higher Ed*. https://www.insidehighered.com/news/admissions/2023/06/12/why-students-opt-out-college?utm_source=Inside+Higher+Ed&utm_campaign=8f4624a2fb-DNU_2021_COPY_02&utm_medium=email&utm_term=0_1fcbc04421-8f4624a2fb-237827861&mc_cid=8f4624a2fb&mc_eid=5176a715a3

Johnson, W. B., & Ridley, C. R. (2004). *The elements of mentoring*. Palgrave Macmillan.

Newman, R. (2021). What will the humanities look like in a decade? *Inside Higher Ed*. https://www.insidehighered.com/views/2021/09/03/how-humanities-canflourish-futureopinion?utm_source=Inside+Higher+Ed&utm_campaign=5a2c6baa4c-DNU_2021_COPY_02&utm_medium=email&utm_term=0_1fcbc04421-5a2c6baa4c-225811137&mc_cid=5a2c6baa4c&mc_eid=c82a6df081

Schanzanbach, D. W., Turner, J. A., & Turner, S. (2023). Raising state minimum wages, lowering community college enrollment. National Bureau of Economic Research. http://www.nber.org/papers/w31540

The Chronicle of Higher Education. (2021). The missing men on campus. The Chronicle of Higher Education, Inc.

1EdTech Foundation. (2021). Digital credentials and competency frameworks: Exploring employer readiness and use in talent management. 1EdTech Foundation and IMS Global Learning Consortium, Inc. https://www.imsglobal.org/sites/default/files/wellspring/Wellspring_II_Employer_Research.pdf

Printed in the United States
by Baker & Taylor Publisher Services